THE CORE QUALITIES OF THE ENNEAGRAM

The *Core Qualities* of the *Enneagram*

DANIEL OFMAN

RITA VAN DER WECK

SCRIPTUM

Published by
Scriptum
Dam 2
3111 BD Schiedam
The Netherlands

Tel: +31-10-427.10.22 Fax: +31-10-473.66.25
e-mail: info@scriptum.nl

This publication is designed to provide accurate and authoritative information in regard to the subject matter covered. It is sold with the understanding that the publisher is not engaged in rendering professional services. If professional advice or other expert assistance is required, the services of a competent professional person should be sought.

Copyright © 2001 Daniel Ofman and Rita van der Weck

All rights reserved. No part of this book may be reproduced or transmitted in any form or by any other means, electronic or mechanical, including photocopying, recording or by any other information storage and retrieval system, without permission from the publishers.

ISBN 90 5594 244 8 / NUGI 684

Contents

Foreword Daniel Ofman 9
Foreword Rita van der Weck 13

Introduction 17
Enneagram types 17 – Centres 20 – Wings 27 – Arrows 29 – Core qualities 32

TYPE ONE The Perfectionist 39
General description of a ONE 41 – Detailed description of a ONE 41 – Core qualities of a ONE 43 – Less healthy aspects of a ONE 45 – Wings of a ONE 45 – A ONE at his/her best 46 – Core quadrants and arrow movements of a ONE 47

TYPE TWO The Helper 49
General description of a TWO 51 – Detailed description of a TWO 51 – Core qualities of a TWO 53 – Less healthy aspects of a TWO 55 – Wings of a TWO 56 – A TWO at his/her best 56 – Core quadrants and arrow movements of a TWO 57

TYPE THREE The Performer 57
General description of a THREE 61 — Detailed description of a THREE 61 — Core qualities of a THREE 63 — Less healthy aspects of a THREE 65 — Wings of a THREE 66 — A THREE at his/her best 66 — Core quadrants and arrow movements of a THREE 67

TYPE FOUR The Individualist 69
General description of a FOUR 71 — Detailed description of a FOUR 71 — Core qualities of a FOUR 75 — Less healthy aspects of a FOUR 75 — Wings of a FOUR 77 — A FOUR at his/her best 77 — Core quadrants and arrow movements of a FOUR 78

TYPE FIVE The Observer 81
General description of a FIVE 83 — Detailed description of a FIVE 83 — Core qualities of a FIVE 87 — Less healthy aspects of a FIVE 88 — Wings of a FIVE 88 — A FIVE at his/her best 89 — Core quadrants and arrow movements of a FIVE 90

TYPE SIX The Loyalist 93
General description of a SIX 95 — Detailed description of a SIX 95 — Core qualities of a SIX 99 — Less healthy aspects of a SIX 99 — Wings of a SIX 100 — A SIX at his/her best 100 — Core quadrants and arrow movements of a SIX 101

TYPE SEVEN The Optimist   103
General description of a SEVEN *105 – Detailed description of a* SEVEN *105 – Core qualities of a* SEVEN *107 – Less healthy aspects of a* SEVEN *109 – Wings of a* SEVEN *109 – A* SEVEN *at his/her best 110 – Core quadrants and arrow movements of a* SEVEN *111*

TYPE EIGHT The Leader   113
General description of an EIGHT *115 – Detailed description of an* EIGHT *115 – Core qualities of an* EIGHT *119 – Less healthy aspects of an* EIGHT *119 – Wings of an* EIGHT *121 – An* EIGHT *at his/her best 121 – Core quadrants and arrow movements of an* EIGHT *122*

TYPE NINE The Mediator   125
General description of a NINE *127 – Detailed description of a* NINE *127 – Core qualities of a* NINE *131 – Less healthy aspects of a* NINE *131 – Wings of a* NINE *132 – A* NINE *at his/her best 132 – Core quadrants and arrow movements of a* NINE *133*

A Test   137
Development Plans   148
Grass   157

Anyway

People are unreasonable, illogical and self-centred.
    Love them anyway.
If you do good, people will accuse you of selfish, ulterior motives.
    Do good anyway.
If you are successful, you will attract false friends and true enemies.
    Succeed anyway.
The good you do will be forgotten tomorrow.
    Do good anyway.
Honesty and frankness make you vulnerable.
    Be honest and frank anyway.
What you spend years building may be destroyed overnight.
    Build anyway.
Give the world the best you have and you'll get kicked in the teeth.
    Give the world the best you've got—anyway.

From "A simple Path" quote from the wall of Shishu Bhavan,
Mother Theresa's children's home in Calcutta

Foreword by Daniel Ofman

"Do you know what you should do? You should make a CD-ROM with Rita van der Weck about the enneagram and core qualities." "What are you on about?" I asked. "Who is Rita, and what have I to do with the enneagram?" It was just before Christmas in 1998 and I had given a lecture at a bank where Theo van der Meent was working at the time. It was my last workday of the year.

Theo is a remarkable character. Since I first met him in 1983, our paths have crossed regularly, every few years or so. He had already encouraged me in the mid-1990s to make a CD-ROM about core qualities. That actually appeared. And now I met him again and he began about the enneagram. I had known about the enneagram for years, but my aversion to preprogrammed models had kept me from really studying it in depth. But because it was the last activity of the year and it was in any case difficult to say 'no' to someone like Theo, I answered somewhat absently: "All right."

And so, in February 1999, I met Rita and through her the enneagram. To say that I was immediately enthralled by the enneagram would be an exaggeration, but the meeting with Rita, Theo and Marc van Seters, whom I had invited, was extremely inspiring. Four totally different people that I would never have brought together, but four who miraculously fitted in with each other and generated together such energy that we decided to go farther.

It was soon evident that together we could set something wonderful in motion and we began to recognise the possibilities. At this stage my interest in the enneagram was roused. And, as I said, I don't feel much for models where you fill in a questionnaire which results in an analysis that tells you how you are. I have seen and tried out so many, varying from management styles (Hersey and Blanchard), learning styles (Kolb), conflict styles (Thomas and Killman), leadership styles (Wilson Learning) and interaction styles (Leary) to the Meyers Briggs Type Indicator, that I begin to wonder what this actually contributes to people's development.

For me it is all about reflection. Questionnaires invite you to react and not to reflect. Thus I was rather sceptical, particularly when, in answering the list of questions, I barely recognised myself. Still, the enneagram intrigued me enough for me to begin studying it in depth. During the investigation I began to let go of my preconceptions and to discover the riches that lie hidden in the model. Thus the idea arose of making a CD-ROM which helps you to write a personal development plan based on the enneagram and core qualities. And with it there ought to be a book as well.

The aim of this book is to make you more aware of what motivates you, why you do the things you do. When you go through this story you have a reasonable indication of your enneagram type. Although it is handy to know what type you are, that is not the primary aim. More important are answers to the questions: What can you do with the knowledge of your own enneagram type and that of the other types? How do you break free of your automatic pilot? What can you do with your free will? How can you liberate yourself?

The uplifting paradox of the enneagram is that, if you examine the difficult aspects of yourself and allow them a place in your life, you become free as a result. If you also keep the characteristics that you do not value in yourself, they can change. Every person is unique. You are unique, your needs are unique and the way in which you express them is unique.

When this book can help you a little along the road to making you more aware of who you actually are deep within, then we have reached our first goal.

Our second goal is to convert this consciousness into concrete active steps, because the world is not waiting on people who are aware of who they are and what their core qualities are. The world needs people who can turn this consciousness to the benefit of their environment, who can take concrete steps that are noticeable for their environment. In other words: the world needs people who have wakened up to make their contribution to the development of this planet. In my first book *Core Qualities: A Gateway to Human Resources** there is on the first page what Howard Thurmon (minister) once said:

> *"Don't ask what the world needs,*
> *Rather ask what makes you come alive;*
> *then go and do it!*
> *Because what the world needs*
> *is people who have come alive."*

May this book help you to come alive and find your own way.

Daniel Ofman

Bussum, Fall 2001

---

* *Core Qualities: A Gateway to Human Resources.*
Schiedam: Scriptum (ISBN 90 5594 240 5)

Foreword by Rita van der Weck

Since my youth I have asked myself questions like: Who am I? Why am I here? What is it all about and why do I do the things I do? In the course of my adult life my search became only more intensive. All the training and courses in the field of personal and professional development provided missing pieces of the puzzle. But these pieces kept taking their places in an ever bigger, more unknown whole. Until I became acquainted with the enneagram.

A new world opened up for me. Thanks to the enneagram I learned to understand my own reactions better. I had more insight into what drove me and who I was. The enneagram describes nine recurrent patterns of thinking, feeling and acting. In order to escape from the prison of these fixed patterns, you must first know what holds you captive. The enneagram lets you see the way to a wider perspective of freer choices. The enneagram makes you aware of how you direct and sometimes fix your attention. And, more important, you learn to see what you pay no attention to and what you could pay attention to.

The enneagram has taught me a great deal about myself and others. And it still does. Seeing yourself as you are, without judging. Looking at your irritations, fears, exaggerations and the things you hide from yourself and others. What a freedom not to have to hide things from yourself, not to have to disclaim anything! That brings peace and power at the same time. I have also noticed that the things in myself that I do not value could be my best qualities. They are simply developed a little too strongly. That is why I am so enthusiastic about the combination of the enneagram and Daniel's core quadrant.

The enneagram is not just of value for personal development. The insights also prove to be of enormous value in organisations. I have led many team-building sessions with the enneagram as the self-awareness model. The result is that more openness, space and understanding for each other are created within a team. The co-operation improves because people learn to look at their automatic patterns with a smile. The glue that fixes these patterns can then be melted. Each and every time it is a fascinating experience. That is why I hope the enneagram will develop further in business life into an instrument for increasing mutual respect and improving co-operative relationships. Being aware of the different personalities in a team can prevent a lot of trouble and suffering and lead to better results for the company.

This brings me to my personal experience last year with Daniel Ofman, Marc van Seters and Theo van der Meent. All four of us are different and single-minded in our own ways. We also went through a growing process. Sometimes we were at our best. Energy flowed and creative ideas came from nowhere. At another time things went less smoothly. And although it was against our will, we also fell into traps of irritation, impatience and criticism. Naturally the enneagram and the core quadrant were at work in our process as well! Partly through this, pleasure always gained the upper hand again before long.

And now it is a year later. The product is ready, the process at an end, or rather at the beginning. I wish much recognition and insight to everyone who goes through the process, in whatever manner. And remember: only you can determine the effect of the core qualities of the enneagram on yourself. Because conscious and subconscious resistance within yourself and the measure to which you are prepared to reflect on yourself and thereby grow, determine the reaction brought about in your case. Wishing you much success and pleasure.

Rita van der Weck

Oudenbosch, Fall 2001

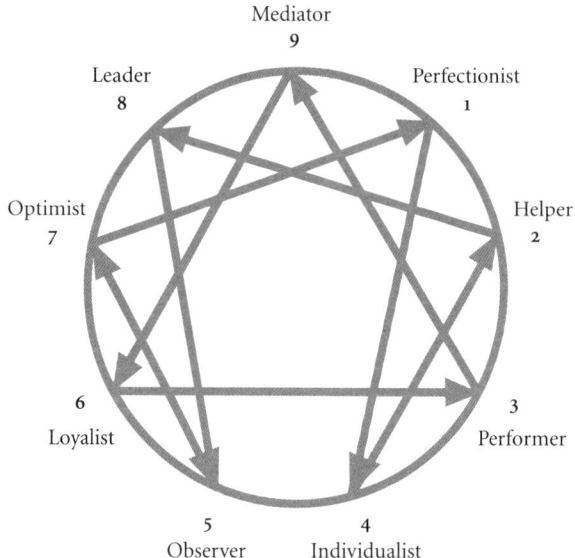

Introduction

Enneagram types

The enneagram is a centuries-old model meaning literally in Greek 'nine' (*ennea)* and 'something drawn or written' (*gram*). It is a dynamic circle which describes the nine personality types and their mutual interactions. Each type has its own strategy leading to success, but also brings limitations with it; nine patterns of thinking, feeling and acting. It is a living model, because in the nine-pointed star, the points 3 – 9 – 6 – 3 are linked to each other by arrows in an equilateral triangle. The remaining points, 1 – 4 – 2 – 8 – 5 – 7 – 1 form with the arrows a hexagon.

It is not quite clear where the enneagram comes from precisely. It is supposed to have originated a few thousand years ago in the Middle East. The insights were passed down by word of mouth from generation to generation. In any event, it is known that it was used for centuries by spiritual schools in a religious context for spiritual development. Nowadays the enneagram is proving its value in such fields as psychology, business, relationships and upbringing.

When someone becomes acquainted with the nine basic

personalities he* will initially find something of himself in every number. The nine types can be conceived as nine lamps. All the lamps are lit but one burns the brightest. That is the basic type. A basic type arises at a very early age. From birth every person begins to notice thoughts, happenings and feelings. These subconscious feelings and thoughts go in all directions. Reason does not work yet and in order to be able to deal with reality everyone subconsciously chooses a survival strategy. For protection one builds all sorts of mechanisms around core qualities. In this way every person begins to form an acquired personality, and as he grows older values, limitations and guilt feelings instilled by tutors and society begin to penetrate. Ideals are internalised and evasion strategies employed to avoid experiencing (again) unpleasant emotions. One conviction piles up on another. In this way fixed patterns are developed when someone notices that these work for him. For instance, if someone realises that it pays to be strong, he will choose a strategy different from a child who notices that he earns the love of his parents by being nice. One develops subconsciously a strategy which is based on the innate possibilities and also strongly influenced by the genes, the upbringing and the culture.

By the time someone is grown up, he is good at hiding his fears, needs and desires. He has made a habit of protect-

---

* In the interests of readability of the text, the authors have opted to write only 'he' wherever 'he or she' is meant. It goes without saying that all the text in this book is intended for both male and female readers.

ing himself. Problems can arise when someone pretends to himself that he is not who he is. The moment you become aware why you do things the way you do, is the beginning of a fascinating transformation process. In this the enneagram is a valuable and accurate aid, because it penetrates to the level of the (usually subconscious) mental and emotional motivation—motives that drive someone from deep within to do the things he does. Every person is driven by a certain core motivation. There are nine main groups of these, which form at the same time the nine basic types of which the enneagram is built up:

1. The *Perfectionist* wants to be good and improve things
2. The *Helper* wants to love or be loved
3. The *Performer* wants to feel valued and accepted
4. The *Individualist* wants to understand who he is and express himself
5. The *Observer* wants to understand the world around him and be competent
6. The *Loyalist* wants certainty and safety
7. The *Optimist* wants to be glad, happy and satisfied
8. The *Leader* wants to protect himself by being strong and full of self-confidence
9. The *Mediator* wants to live in unity and harmony with others.

Centres

We are all linked to the world by our instinct, our feelings and our thinking. That means that we experience life in many different ways. Even so you can speak generally of three forms of consciousness: physical, emotional and mental. Every one of us has access to all three. However, everyone has, as a result of his own personality, a preference for one of the three. The nine personalities of the enneagram are divided into these three groups, also called the 'centres'. Each person has his centre of gravity in one of the three centres. In the centre that someone has developed the most lies his strong side, and at the same time his pitfall. Whenever one of the three centres predominates, the harmony is broken.

The FIVE, SIX and SEVEN are the mental types in the intellectual centre (head). Each of these three personalities experiences the world as an overwhelming, fearsome or limiting place. Their energy seems to be turned inward: the FIVE isolates himself in his thoughts, the SIX withdraws carefully before he either escapes from a possible danger or actually throws himself into it. The SEVEN withdraws from present commitment and activities in his constant search for new stimuli.

People from the emotional centre (heart)—TWO, THREE and FOUR—are also called the 'heart people', because the heart is traditionally seen as the seat of the emotions. The energy of these three types goes out towards others in order to be able to sound out emotions. The TWO wants love, the THREE admiration and the FOUR wants to be understood.

EIGHT, NINE and ONE, the people in the gut-instinct centre (abdominal), experience—whenever a situation arises—bodily sensations first before they are able to think or to feel. These sensations are often felt in the abdominal region. The energy of these gut-instinct types is the energy to take up a position of resistance somewhere. This manifests itself in the EIGHT in aggressiveness, in the NINE in obstinacy and in a critical perfectionism in the ONE.

Head—the intellectual centre
The intellectual centre is the seat of the mental intelligence. The intellectual centre has to do with our thinking. Head-orientated types tend to approach life via their thinking. They have a lively imagination and an exceptional talent for analysing mental images and making connections between them.

In every situation head types first take a step back, as it were, to consider and survey everything. They must first orientate themselves and think things over. Only then are feeling and acting the order of the day. They experience life via mental impressions. They need a logical system in which things have meaning and purpose. Within that they can then include everything and establish order in what is or seems to be chaotic. They have the tendency to take everything literally. In their approach to life they hang fire, first listening and thinking attentively, and only then acting—like a solo violinist who first listens attentively to the orchestra to determine the correct beat and tempo, and only then begins to play. The most important aspect is attaining an objective vision. They have a large inner world full of thoughts, plans, dreams and fears. Head types often experience strong emotions, but express these with difficulty. The primary emotion is fear and the primary thought is suspicion.

Heart—the emotional centre
The emotional centre is the seat of the emotional intelligence. In the emotional centre we experience emotions: the wordless sensations that tell us how we feel, as opposed to our opinion about something. Heart-orientated types go through the world via relationships. They quickly understand someone else's needs and moods and react to them (consciously or subconsciously).

Heart types experience their intuitive impressions via their emotions. They are often people who are overly busy and physically active. They are intensely involved in the world around them. It is important for them to understand others and to be there for others. This centre revolves round feelings, emotions and relationships. The way outward for them is perfectly natural. They react to stimuli and signals that impinge on them and to judgements and expectations from outside. You can compare them to a violin, whose strings are played on by life. Approval by others is important for them. Because they tend to adapt to the needs of others or to go along with what others want them to be, it is sometimes difficult (for themselves and for others) to know what is genuine and what is imitative in their behaviour. Image plays a major role.

The primary emotion is sorrow and the primary thought is confusion.

Abdomen—the gut-instinct centre
The gut-instinct centre is the seat of our intuitive intelligence, where we sense our physical 'being', as opposed to our thoughts and feelings. Via this centre we experience ourselves physically *vis-à-vis* other people and our environment. It is the source of our energy and gives us the power to be active in the physical environment.

Gut-instinct types perceive via their bodies above all. They react instinctively, swiftly and directly and are often swept along with their immediate reaction. Feeling good is important. What they feel determines their actions and thinking to a large extent. They have difficulty in conforming to standard patterns and prefer to decide on the beat of the music themselves. Patience is not their strongest side. Power and control play—sometimes subconsciously—a major role. They want to know who is in charge. Depending on others is difficult. They defend their territory. They fly the flags of honesty and justice high. However, they take the law into their own hands easily.

The primary emotion is anger and the primary thought is self-forgetting.

From the intellectual centre someone says:

I am interested in thinking, calculating and weighing up things.

I believe that there is a basic order in life.

In new situations I prefer to keep my distance at first in order to think before I act.

I tend to think there are always more things to be learned.

I presume that if I am aware of anything, then others are too.

I have the tendency to work hard in order to know more.

I am often afraid of not knowing enough, so that I either ask questions or keep quiet.

When I am in a new situation I am careful until I am sure of myself.

I am often afraid to talk about things I am not sure of.

I often feel more at ease with people who think the same as I do.

I tend to become entangled in considering endless possibilities.

I have the urge to look for the meaning of everything.

I am content in my inner world, and when I leave it I know I can always return to it.

It is easy for me to forget my body when I am absorbed by my world of ideas.

I feel at ease in a world of thoughts and ideas.

Information is essential for me in order to be prepared.

I don't have to do anything with what I learn.

I have more questions than I could ever ask.

Sometimes I am not sure whether I should wait or go into action.

The more information I have, the surer I feel.

From the emotional centre someone says:

I am interested in feelings, emotions and relationships.

I tend to be restless when I have nothing to do.

Often I don't know what I feel.

I am conscious of what impression I make on others.

It is important for me to look good in the eyes of others.

I have the tendency to compare myself with others.

I feel uneasy when I have no job to do.

Life is a network of relationships.

I sometimes look to others for indications that tell me how well I am doing something

I like it when others say I am doing something well.

I have the tendency to think ahead about the next thing I must do.

I like to help others by bringing them in contact with the right people.

I want to be seen as someone who matters.

It is important for me to feel attached to other people.

When I learn something I think about how I could use it.

I tend to make projects of everything.

Sometimes I think I can make my body do what I want.

I have to get away from my usual surroundings in order to take it easier.

Something inside me tells me sometimes that I cannot measure up to other people.

I recognise confusion in my life.

From the gut-instinct centre someone says:

I am interested in safety, instinctive reactions and existence.

When I experience something intensely, I can be totally wrapped up in it.

One of the worst things that can happen to me is to fall slightly short.

Usually I know immediately if I like something or not.

I fight only for something that has value for me.

I sense who holds the power in a certain situation.

Usually I feel it when something is amiss.

Nothing that is worthwhile comes without trouble.

I am my body.

I tend to consider something in moral terms: is it good or bad?

I like people to be clear.

When my emotions surface, I am afraid to lose control.

Being vulnerable means for me giving someone control over myself.

When I meet people I decide if I will spend energy on them or not.

I tend to deny things until I have heard them various times.

I usually take care that I remain the master of every situation.

I have the idea that life is a struggle.

If my feelings become too strong, I am afraid I will be carried away by them.

I do not give ground quickly and I find it important to have power and influence.

Head people are little aware of their bodies. Heart people generally have problems with analysing their emotions logically and gut-instinct people with experiencing and expressing their emotions.
- Head people think first, then feel and act last.
- Heart people feel first, then act and think last.
- Gut-instinct people act first, then think and feel last.

That brings us to an interesting starting-point. By seeing the centre as part of a circular footpath, someone can clockwise create harmony in his life. In other words, what can you learn or use from the centre that lies before you?

It revolves round harmony among the three centres and generally speaking development lies in striking a balance. The following applies to the three centres:
- Intellectual centre: developing a balance between thinking and acting (gut-instinct centre).
- Emotional centre: developing a balance between feeling and thinking (intellectual centre).
- Gut-instinct centre: developing a balance between acting and feeling (emotional centre).

Wings

Nobody is a pure enneagram type: everyone is a unique mix of his basic type and the wings. The wings fill in the colour of the enneagram type. They lie directly left and right of one's own enneagram number. The fact that you have two wings as enneagram type offers help in finding your own enneagram number. If you are just beginning with the enneagram, you often switch to and fro between two or three numbers that lie close to another: your enneagram type and your wings.

A number of theories exist on how the wings of your type function. In general most of us have developed a dominant wing. There are also, however, enneagram types with strong influences from both wings, or types that are hardly influenced by their wings at all. It can even be so that your wing partner is so strongly developed that the characteristics of this wing come out stronger than those of your basic type—further proof that we are all unique.

You can regard your wing as the sub-type of your basic type. If you look at your own personality you will perhaps recognise that you tend towards the one thing more often than towards the other. Through the influence of your wing, you will recognise many of these traits. Thus a TWO with a ONE wing will recognise much of the perfectionist—only never really as pure as a perfectionist goes through life.

If you want insight into your wing characteristics, then read first of all the description of the two enneagram numbers directly left and right of your type. With which do you feel the most or the least associated? Or do you have the strong characteristics of both? Observe yourself and your patterns objectively and honestly, and read how the wings add nuances to the enneagram types.

Arrows

If you look at the enneagram, each type is linked with two other enneagram numbers by an arrow. The lines (arrows) first link the points 9 – 6 – 3 – 9 and thereafter 1 – 4 – 2 – 8 – 5 – 7 – 1 with each other. Each enneagram type has two partners. These have a different effect on the personality. Most of us have a preferred pattern in which we look for our escape if we are under pressure. It is good to know what your patterns are. Being aware of your patterns can help you—whenever you want—to make other choices.

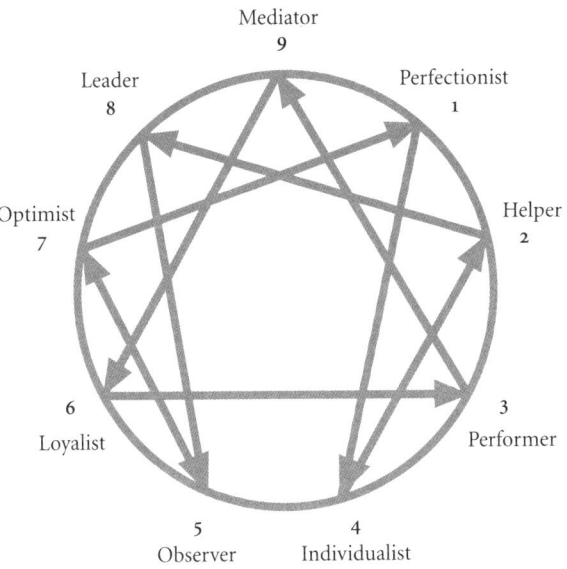

Under pressure, if you do not feel good, you go almost automatically in the direction of the arrows and shoot towards the one partner, your disintegration point. There is then a tendency to make free with the negative qualities of this enneagram number. If you feel good, you go in the direction opposite to the arrow towards your other arrow partner, your integration point. Working towards this integration point is obviously not as easy as shooting towards the disintegration point. Awareness and patience are needed for this. By being aware of your integration point you can admit the positive qualities of this enneagram type and then you will discover many new possibilities and talents in yourself.

Movement to disintegration

For every type the movement towards disintegration is via the sequence of the numbers 1 – 4 – 2 – 8 – 5 – 7 – 1. This therefore means that types in their average to unhealthy state will display a few of the average or unhealthy behavioural aspects of their type of stress. For instance, an average to unhealthy Perfectionist will let some average to unhealthy behavioural aspects of the FOUR be seen, heard, or felt. An average to unhealthy Helper will display a few average to unhealthy qualities of the EIGHT, and so forth.

In the equilateral triangle the sequence with disintegration is 9 – 6 – 3 – 9. An average to unhealthy NINE will sometimes behave like an average to unhealthy SIX and an average to unhealthy SIX can take over the less positive qualities of the THREE, and a THREE the same in turn from the NINE.

Movement in integration

The movement in integration for every type is the opposite to that for disintegration. With integration the movement is 1 – 7 – 5 – 8 – 2 – 4 – 1.

If he is relaxed the Perfectionist will display healthy qualities of the SEVEN, a relaxed SEVEN gains access to the positive qualities of the FIVE, the FIVE to those of the EIGHT, and so forth until the circle closes again (or opens) with the FOUR, who goes in the process of integration to the ONE.

In the equilateral triangle the sequence 9 – 3 – 6 – 9 is: a relaxed NINE gains access to the positive qualities of the THREE, a THREE goes to the SIX and the SIX in his turn to the NINE again.

The influences of the movements in integration and disintegration are, irrespective of the personality type, important. Thus, when you know what basic type you are, you can find out which other enneagram numbers influence you. To build up a full picture of yourself you can include in your observation the qualities of your basic type, your wing(s) and the movements in integration and disintegration.

In stressful situations other emotions come to the surface than in periods when you are happy and self-assured. Just look and see what arrow movements you recognise. Just consider how your personality changes if you feel very good, happy and relaxed. And naturally, in the opposite situation, if it is not going well with you and you feel angry, for instance, or unhappy, how do you change then?

Core qualities

Core qualities are those which belong to the being (the core) of a type. Thus you can distinguish a number of core qualities in every enneagram type. Core qualities 'colour' a person; it is the specific strength we immediately think of with someone. Examples of core qualities are decisiveness, consideration, carefulness, susceptibility, orderliness, the ability to gauge feelings, and so forth. A core quality can be recognised in someone's exceptional skill, of which he himself says: "But everyone can do that".

A core quality is always potentially present. You cannot switch a core quality on or off at will, but you can keep it hidden. The difference between qualities and behaviour lies first and foremost in the fact that qualities come from within and behaviour is acquired. Behaviour can therefore be learned; qualities can be developed. The clearer the picture is of the core qualities we have, the more consciously we can let those illuminate our work.

Just as there can be no light without dark, so too has every core quality a sunny and a shadowy side. The shadowy side is sometimes called the distortion. The distortion is not the opposite of the core quality (as active is the opposite of passive and strong the opposite of weak). The distortion is what a core quality becomes if it goes too far. Thus a core quality 'helpfulness' can go too far and become 'interference'. Then the strength of the enneagram type becomes the weakness.

In colloquial terms this is known as 'too much of a good thing' and that expresses it precisely. Someone who is too careful runs the risk of becoming fussy. In the same way the ability to adapt can go too far and be seen as fickleness. The flexible person will then have this thrown at him regularly as a reproach.

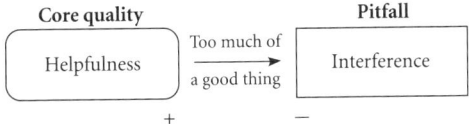

The distortion of someone's core quality is at the same time his 'pitfall'. The pitfall is that which the person concerned often has stuck on him as a label. Then the person with the quality decisiveness is reproached and told he should not push so much. Whether that is justified or not, the pitfall belongs to the core quality. They are linked inseparably with each 1other in every enneagram type.

With the corresponding pitfall the person receives in his core quality also his 'challenge'. The challenge is the positive opposite quality of the pitfall. The positive opposite quality of pushiness is something like patience or restraint. In other words, the challenge 'patience' belongs to the pitfall 'pushiness'. As is clear in the diagram, the core quality and the challenge are each other's complementary qualities.

What matters is finding the balance between decisiveness and patience. When this balance tips too far over to decisiveness, then there is a chance that this decisiveness goes too far and becomes pushiness. In other words, to prevent one landing in one's pitfall, it is advisable to develop the challenge. That applies to each of the nine enneagram types.

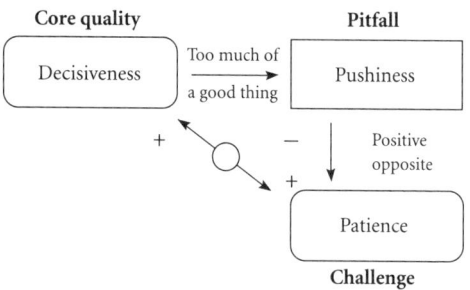

Striking a balance means thinking in terms of 'and–and' and not of 'either–or'. The art for this person is to be, at the same time, decisive and patient as well. Thus it is not about becoming less decisive, because otherwise you run the risk of pushing; it is about patient decisiveness. Someone who is patiently decisive no longer runs the risk of pushing; that is a logical consequence of the fact that both qualities are two sides of one coin. The difficulty often lies in the fact that the one involved is not in a position to see how these two qualities can go together, that is to say, it is a question for him of either decisiveness or patience. For him both qualities are more opposites than complements.

As already said, it can often be deduced from someone's core quality where the potential conflicts with the environment can be expected. Those often have to do with his challenge. The problem is namely that the average person seems to be allergic to an overdose of his challenge, particularly if he finds it in another personification. Thus the decisive person will tend to lose his self-control when confronted with passivity in another. He is allergic to passivity because passivity is too much of his challenge (= patience). Often he does not know how to handle it.

The more someone is confronted with his own allergy in another, the greater is the chance that he will end up in his pitfall. The person with the core quality 'decisiveness' then runs the risk of pushing even more while he reproaches the other person with being passive, and so forth. In other words: if one encounters one's allergy in another, the pitfall lies in wait. Thus what makes someone most vulnerable is not his pitfall, but his allergy, for it is the allergy more than anything that pushes someone into his pitfall.

The core quadrant is not just an aid in discovering core qualities and challenges in yourself and others. What a core

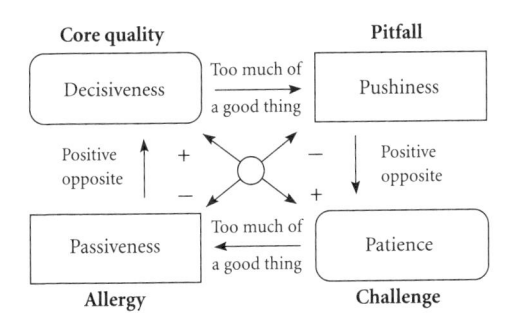

Core quality		Pitfall
Decisiveness	Too much of a good thing →	Pushiness
Positive opposite ↑ + −		− ↓ Positive opposite +
Passiveness	← Too much of a good thing	Patience
Allergy		Challenge

quadrant also lets you see is that it is very well possible for you to learn most from those who irritate you most (people for whom you have an allergy), or to put it another way: "What you are allergic to in another, is probably too much of something good that you yourself actually need most. Thus you can learn most from those with whom you get along least."

Every enneagram type has a number of specific qualities. The most obvious are the following:

1. The Perfectionist: self-discipline trustworthiness, orderliness, idealism
2. The Helper: helpfulness, sensitivity for relationships, enthusiasm, tact
3. The Performer: passion, purposefulness, optimism, resolution
4. The Individualist: introspection, sympathy, sensitivity, ardour
5. The Observer: shrewdness, independence, contemplation, calmness
6. The Loyalist: alertness, loyalty, seriousness, responsibility
7. The Optimist: spontaneity, charm, light-heartedness, curiosity
8. The Leader: belligerence, directness, authority, courage
9. The Mediator: restfulness, toleration, susceptibility, cautiousness

In a core quadrant it can also be seen how a person tends to react when stressed or under pressure. In the first instance the pressure or stress will lead to the person showing more often too much of a good thing, in other words he will run into his pitfall. If the pressure becomes still greater, then he will tend (unexpectedly) to overshoot into his allergy and indulge in it. These are the moments when the environment no longer recognises someone. The behaviour that he or she then shows is so unusual for those around that incomprehension arises. Someone who is 'normally' speaking very courageous, very decisive and is regarded in his environment as energetic will become in the first place a little too bold and thereafter, under stress, will behave hesitatingly and indecisively.

From the enneagram can be seen what the various types tend to do under stress and how one type under stress has the tendency, via the arrow movement, to take on the pitfall of another type.

This also applies when a type feels good and develops himself. When he becomes more balanced he will tend to take on the core quality of another type.

In this way a number of core quadrants can be linked with each other so that one can see the mutual influences of the various types.

Type ❶ *The Perfectionist*

"*While others can surrender themselves to the sound colour of the whole orchestra, my hair very soon stands on end because to my ears only the missers come to the foreground. The annoying thing is that I know exactly in my head how a score like that should sound. That's just what is so irritating.*

"*Something is right or something is wrong and as far as I'm concerned there's nothing in between. And if it's right it can probably always be better.*"

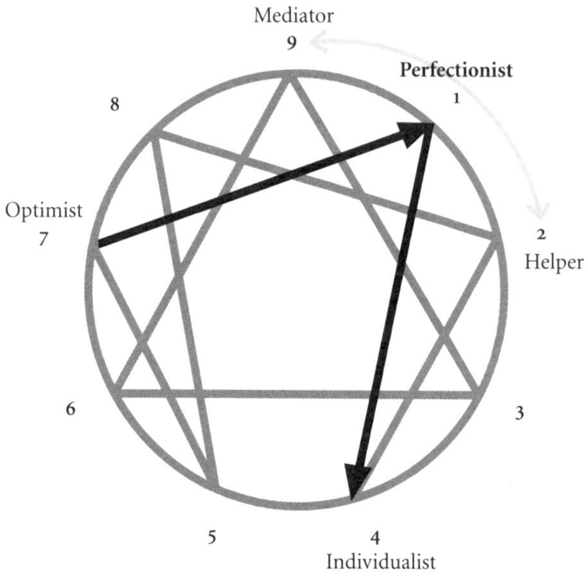
Mediator
9
Perfectionist
1
8
Optimist
7
2
Helper
6
3
5
4
Individualist

General description of a ONE
I have a strong feeling for what is right and what is wrong. My eye falls directly on things that can be improved. I understand immediately what is going wrong and know what is needed to set that right. I do things with the greatest possible care and perhaps because of this I can hardly stand it when others do them half-heartedly. Some find me critical. So I am, and most of all with myself. I can also come across as something of a smart aleck. That is not my intention; it is just that I know how things can be done best.

Detailed description of a ONE
If I had to describe myself I would say first how important I find it to do things well. I have a kind of inner drive to improve things. I see immediately when something is wrong. And something is right or it isn't; there's nothing between. You can call me the eternal perfectionist. I feel how things ought to be. My problem is that I find it difficult to accept that people and situations are often not as they should be. I stumble constantly over the imperfections in the lives of others, and above all in myself. That irritates me. I must

hold my irritation off, because I find it annoying if someone sees in me that I am angry. Earlier I just learned that I have to be kind and good. That is why I want to keep under control everything to do with the irritations, stress and emotions that live within me. I'm afraid that if I don't do that I will lose my control over them.

I am critical, towards myself and others. I set high standards—things can always be better. Within me is a little voice that tells me constantly that things are still not good enough. A voice that criticises everything and everyone, myself above all. I often discuss with this voice how things are and how they ought to be.

I can't accept vagueness. Forgiving is difficult for me. I can be hard if people do their work carelessly or cut corners. I can also come over strong and tell everyone how it should be done.

I am not really a social type. I find people are all right but I can't adapt myself so well and have to make an effort to be sociable and remain open for another.

The word 'must' plays a big role in my life. I am always thinking 'it ought to …'. If I believe that something must be so, then it has to be so and nothing else. That means that I often worry about things, organise things, improve things. Letting things take their course is difficult for me.

In my vision of life my viewpoint is that there is a right way to do things, and I want to teach others this. The most important values I stand for are integrity and honesty. I am convinced that what you do, you have to do well.

I often ask myself such questions as: What is honest and what dishonest? My image of myself is that I am right.

My primary motivation is that I want to be good and improve things. My secondary motives drive me:
- To prevent criticism and avoid imperfection
- To aspire to a feeling of perfection and to strive for the ideal
- To treat others fairly and to make the world better
- To keep everything under control, so that no mistakes are made to make sure that I cannot be blamed for anything.

My fear is that there is something wrong with me. That is why I long to be good, yes, even perfect. That is why I focus on the correct performance of duties and the quality of work. The colour that suits me best is silver (cool, sober, clear). The Stabiliser appeals to me most as a leadership style.

No wonder that, apart from Perfectionist, they sometimes call me reformer, improver, completer or judge.

Core qualities of a ONE

Positive characteristics of mine are: serious, responsible, dedicated, just, principled, honest, trustworthy, self-disciplined, organised, orderly, conscientious, idealistic, productive, reasonable, deliberate, loyal, ethical. My core qualities are: self-discipline, trustworthiness, orderliness, idealism.

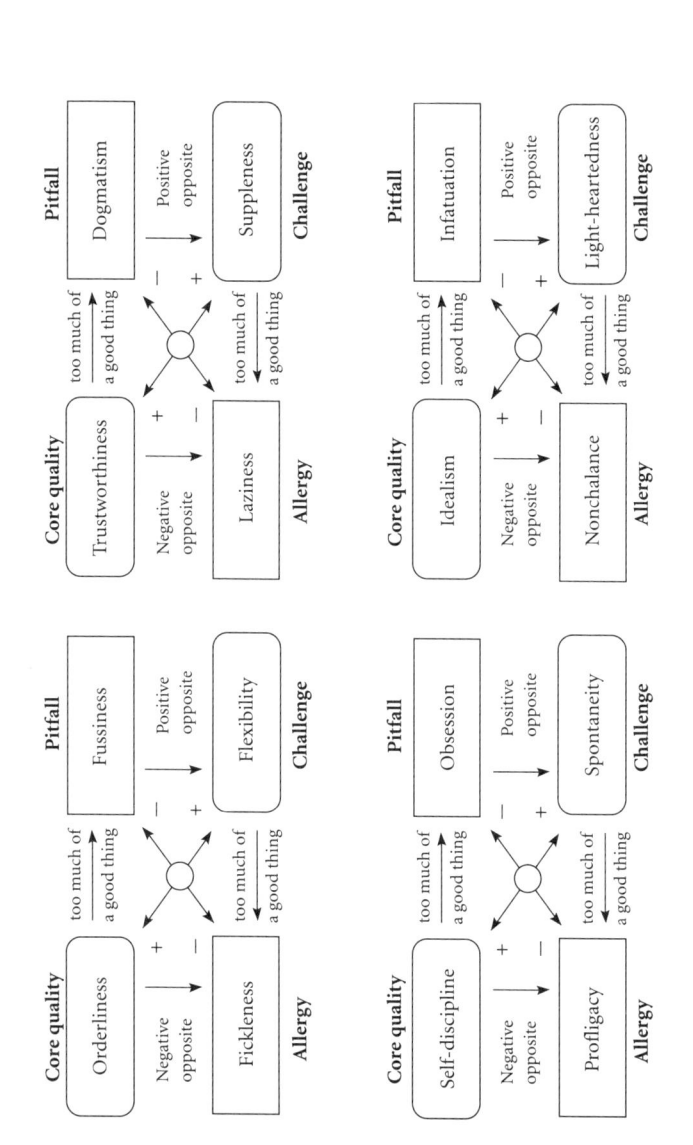

Core quality — Orderliness
Negative opposite → Fickleness — **Allergy**

Pitfall — Fussiness
Positive opposite → Flexibility — **Challenge**

too much of a good thing / too much of a good thing

Core quality — Trustworthiness
Negative opposite → Laziness — **Allergy**

Pitfall — Dogmatism
Positive opposite → Suppleness — **Challenge**

too much of a good thing / too much of a good thing

Core quality — Self-discipline
Negative opposite → Profligacy — **Allergy**

Pitfall — Obsession
Positive opposite → Spontaneity — **Challenge**

too much of a good thing / too much of a good thing

Core quality — Idealism
Negative opposite → Nonchalance — **Allergy**

Pitfall — Infatuation
Positive opposite → Light-heartedness — **Challenge**

too much of a good thing / too much of a good thing

44

Less healthy aspects of a ONE

The less positive characteristics of a ONE are that he is critical, demanding, stiff, formal and impatient. He is allergic to incompetence and unfair criticism. He 'has to…' a lot, can be too serious, inflexible and sermonising, even moralistic or intolerant. Rage and wrath can occasionally be felt under his perfectionism. What he avoids is letting his anger be seen. Where he can be obsessive is in his perfectionism. His defence mechanism is reaction formation. For instance, when he experiences annoyance there is an inner censorship whereby these feelings are suppressed. For him that has become the way not to express his rage directly and to let off his steam in another manner. The defence mechanism prevents the ONE from becoming conscious of inadequacy, imperfection.

When the Perfectionist is under pressure and becomes stressed, he tends to display the less positive characteristics of the FOUR. He can become moody, querulous, (melo)-dramatic, dejected, depressive and unstable. He will readily condemn others who do not live in line with his ideals. The antidote that will help him most to break through well-worn patterns is serenity.

Wings of a ONE

A Perfectionist with a developed TWO wing is probably warmer, more helpful, more critical and more dominating. A Perfectionist with a more developed NINE wing is often more harmony-orientated, is more objective and more relaxed and keeps his distance a little more easily.

A ONE at his best

It gives a Perfectionist a feeling of fulfilment if something works or is as it ought to be. When relaxed the Perfectionist has access to the positive characteristics of the Optimist. There is more acceptance of imperfection. That makes the Perfectionist more relaxed, more optimistic, more spontaneous and more extrovert. In his work he can say to himself: I am all right, even though I am not perfect. He does not take himself and situations so seriously. He comes in contact with his spontaneous side and lets things run their course more than wanting to control them. That means that he becomes more flexible and adapts himself better to changes in the environment.

At his best the Perfectionist values the talents of his workers and stimulates a feeling of togetherness among his team members by ensuring that they satisfy the standards and that they work correctly according to established procedures. Competent workers with the necessary technical knowledge may make decisions in their own field of expertise. As long as the team members are on course and follow the rules, the Perfectionist is inclined to delegate responsibility and loosen his hold on the strings. He has learned to handle his irritation and anger better and to express these instead of letting them build up. He also has more contact with his emotions and with the things he wants instead of 'must do'.

A healthy ONE has become aware that there are other ways than the only right one.

Core quadrants and arrow movements of a ONE

The relationships a ONE has with his arrow movements can be summarised in the following three core quadrants.

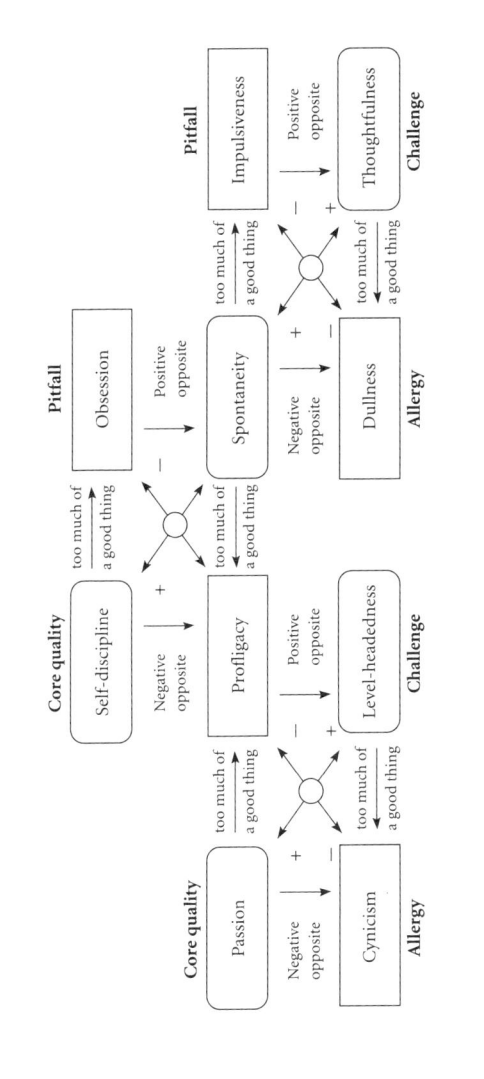

Type One

Core quality: Self-discipline → **Pitfall**: Obsession
Spontaneity (Positive opposite of Obsession; Negative opposite leads to Dullness)
Dullness — **Allergy**

Pitfall: Impulsiveness → Thoughtfulness (Positive opposite) — **Challenge**

Core quality: Passion → Profligacy (too much of a good thing)
Level-headedness (Positive opposite) — **Challenge**
Cynicism — **Allergy** (Negative opposite of Passion)

TYPE ONE under pressure gets the pitfall of
TYPE FOUR The Individualist

TYPE ONE in balance gets the quality of
TYPE SEVEN The Optimist

47

Type ❷ The Helper

"I try to let a client see the human being behind the waiter, as it were. Sometimes I seem just like a social worker. Do you know that there are clients who come here just for me? Surely you can't be paid a bigger compliment than that. I find that very moving."

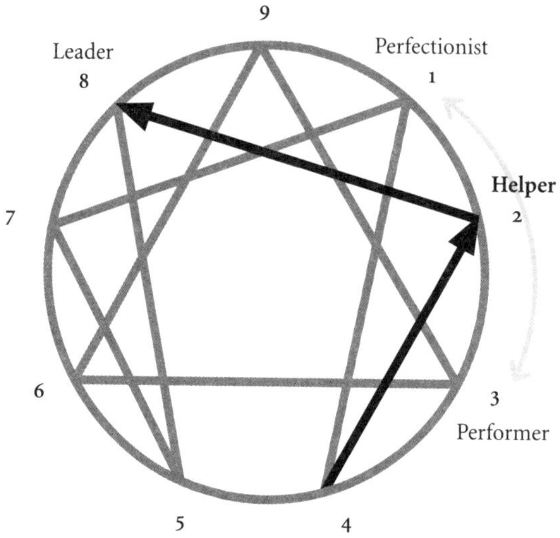
9
Perfectionist
1
Leader
8
Helper
2
7
6
3
Performer
5
4

General description of a TWO

I am always ready to help others and I give easily. I know what people need. I have difficulty saying 'no'. It pleases me when people who are important to me like me. I am more orientated to relationships than to goals. Good relations are therefore very important for me. I can get on with people well and make friends easily. Intimacy and close connections play an important role. I have many different kinds of friends and can easily adapt to the person I am with. I don't find it easy to ask for something myself and have difficulty in receiving things.

Detailed description of a TWO

I like to see myself as someone who wants to be busy on behalf of others. Someone who jumps in where help is needed. It pleases me if I get attention and appreciation from others as a result. I am sympathetic and feel for people. It seems as if I sense what other people feel, what they need—so strongly, in fact, that I identify myself with the other. Then I have to learn to keep some distance and to define my own boundaries. I do not willingly let myself be helped. Anyway, I am not all that conscious of what I need myself. I find it difficult to know what my own desires and needs are. It is even more difficult for me to make these known to another. That makes me dependent and weak.

Without being conscious of it, I am pleased when people appreciate my help. Consequently I find it annoying when people take my help for granted.

I hate every form of violence. For me, hurting others or being hurt myself is awful. I have difficulty admitting to myself that I am angry. I'd rather say I am offended or disappointed. On occasion, if I am really upset, I can seem a bit hysterical. I am not in very good contact with my body. Growing tired is not an option.

Connection with people I care about is very important for me—feeling a bond with them. What matters to me is that people accept me as I am, not because of what I do. For me it has to do with emotional contact. I want to get to know others to their innermost depths. But the strange thing is that I have difficulty in really revealing myself to others. I am more occupied with what goes on in others than with looking within myself and experiencing what goes on there as regards needs and desires. I have to learn not to orientate myself constantly towards the expectations of others and learn to come home to myself. Another important point for my development is that I learn to ask things for myself.

In my vision of life my viewpoint is supporting and strengthening other people; it is fine when people need me.

The most important values I stand for are connection with people and freedom. I am convinced that the needs of people in the organisation are important.

I often ask myself such questions as: What do others need and how can I win their approval? My image of myself is: I am helpful. My primary motivation is that I want to be loved. My secondary motives drive me:
- To be loving and helpful and be appreciated for it
- To strive to be needed and to have an important influence on others
- To be intimate with others and give expression to the feelings I have for others
- To have control over people, so that they like me
- To justify the desires people have *vis-à-vis* others.

My fear is that I am unwanted or unworthy of being loved. That is why I long to mean something. I focus, therefore, on human needs, service and service provision. The colour that suits me best is red (zestful, powerful, passionate). The Counsellor appeals to me most as leadership style.

No wonder that, apart from Helper, they also call me giver, assistant, power behind the throne, or mother.

Core qualities of a TWO
Positive characteristics of mine are: accepting, love-giving, supporting, giving and creative, considerate, complimentary, flexible, co-operative, receptive, empathetic, warm,

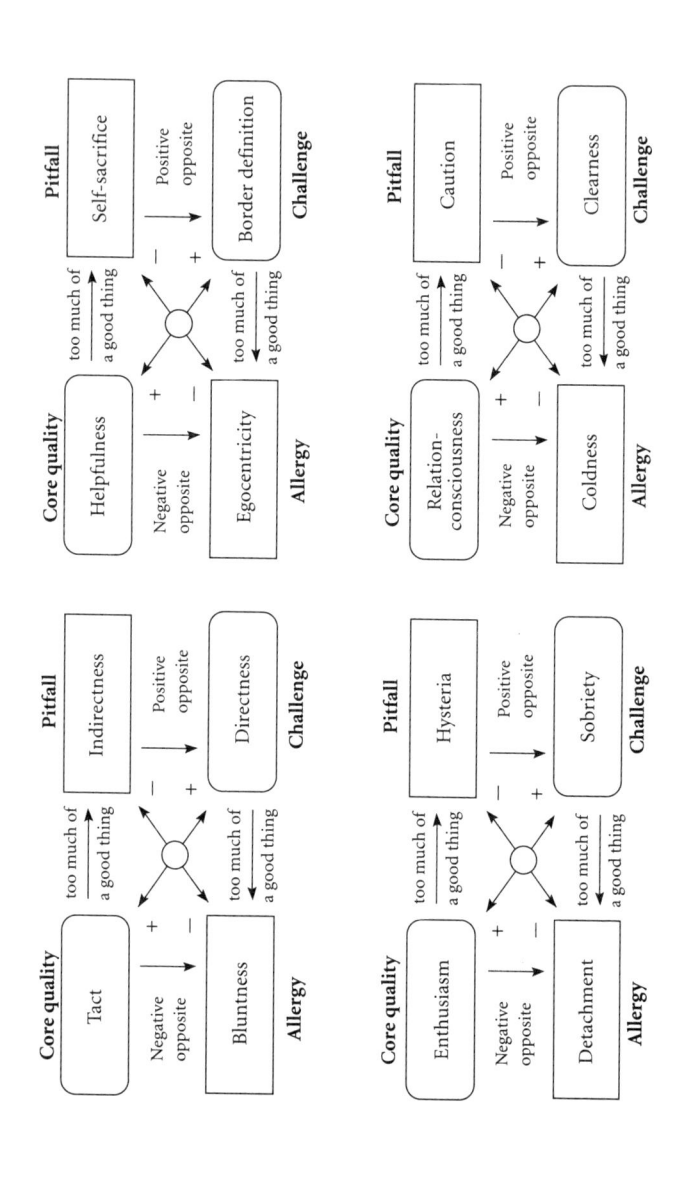

Core quality: Tact

- **Pitfall**: Indirectness
- **Positive opposite** → **Challenge**: Directness
- **Negative opposite** → **Allergy**: Bluntness

Tact (+) → Indirectness (too much of a good thing)
Tact (−) → Bluntness (negative opposite)
Bluntness (+) → Directness (too much of a good thing)

Core quality: Helpfulness

- **Pitfall**: Self-sacrifice
- **Positive opposite** → **Challenge**: Border definition
- **Negative opposite** → **Allergy**: Egocentricity

Helpfulness (+) → Self-sacrifice (too much of a good thing)
Helpfulness (−) → Egocentricity (negative opposite)
Egocentricity (+) → Border definition (too much of a good thing)

Core quality: Enthusiasm

- **Pitfall**: Hysteria
- **Positive opposite** → **Challenge**: Sobriety
- **Negative opposite** → **Allergy**: Detachment

Enthusiasm (+) → Hysteria (too much of a good thing)
Enthusiasm (−) → Detachment (negative opposite)
Detachment (+) → Sobriety (too much of a good thing)

Core quality: Relation-consciousness

- **Pitfall**: Caution
- **Positive opposite** → **Challenge**: Clearness
- **Negative opposite** → **Allergy**: Coldness

Relation-consciousness (+) → Caution (too much of a good thing)
Relation-consciousness (−) → Coldness (negative opposite)
Coldness (+) → Clearness (too much of a good thing)

generous, romantic and understanding. My core qualities are helpfulness, relation-consciousness, enthusiasm and tact.

Less healthy aspects of a TWO

The less positive characteristics of a TWO are that he can be meddlesome, possessive, complaining, needy and jealous. He is allergic to rejection and lack of appreciation. Sometimes he is exaggeratedly friendly or over-protective, suffocating or with the tendency to play the role of victim or to identify himself with the underdog. Underneath his role as helper a certain pride can be felt.

What he avoids is making his own needs known or being needy. And where he can be obsessive is in flattery or wanting to make others content. His defence mechanism is repression. Helpers who are always ready for others have to put their own desires in second place and repress them. This defence mechanism prevents the TWO from being aware of his own needs.

Under pressure or stressed the Helper tends to overshoot towards the Leader and to display there the Leader's less positive characteristics. In order to have his way he can become hostile, manipulating, openly aggressive, domineering, intimidating and demanding. Then he tends to judge others who do not give as much as himself. The antidote that can help him most to break through well-worn patterns is humility and submissiveness.

Wings of a TWO

A Helper with a ONE wing is probably more idealistic, more objective and more (self-)critical than the Helper with a stronger THREE wing. He will also be readier to pass judgements. The Helper with a strong THREE wing is more self-assured, more ambitious, more extrovert and slightly more orientated towards success in the outside world.

A TWO at his best

What gives a Helper a feeling of fulfilment is being needed, and winning approval and acknowledgement.

When the Helper is relaxed and happy he has access to the positive characteristics of the Individualist. There is created awareness of his own needs and emotions, self-acceptance, personal uniqueness and contact with himself. Such characteristics as sensitivity, intuition and intensity are strengthened. He learns to do something for himself without thinking too much about someone else.

In his work he remunerates his own needs just as well as those of others. He teaches others to ask for help directly instead of in an indirect manner, namely by helping others. A healthy Helper can say to himself: I am special and my needs are just as important as those of others. He learns to make room for himself and to express his emotions. He develops a consistent 'self' that does not change in order to fulfil the needs of others and learns to deal on the basis of equality. He says 'no' when it is 'no' and 'yes' when he really means it.

At his best he encourages his team members in developing their talents and skills by advising them how they can do their work well. Training, counselling and coaching are stimulated in order to help workers to develop their talents. He keeps a disciplined focus on things in order to round off tasks, and he holds in balance his own unique worth as a person and the quality of supportive leadership. A healthy TWO has learned to separate his own worth from the approval of others.

Core quadrants and arrow movements of a TWO

The relationships a TWO has with his arrow movements can be summarised in the following three core quadrants. (See figure on next page.)

Type Two

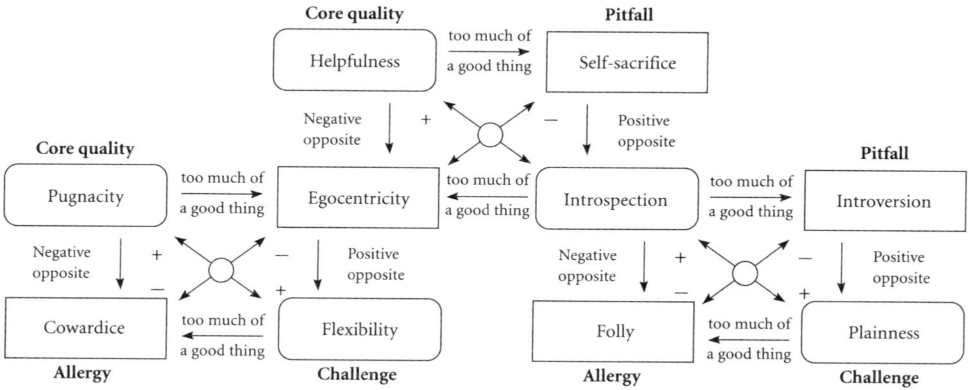

Core quality — Helpfulness → (Negative opposite) → Egocentricity ← **Pitfall** Self-sacrifice (Positive opposite)

Pitfall Self-sacrifice → (Negative opposite) → Folly ← Introspection (Positive opposite of Self-sacrifice)

Pitfall Introversion → Plainness **Challenge** (Positive opposite)

Egocentricity → Flexibility **Challenge** (Positive opposite)

Core quality Pugnacity → (Negative opposite) → Cowardice **Allergy**

Introspection / Folly **Allergy**

(too much of a good thing / too much of a good thing)

TYPE TWO under pressure gets the pitfall of TYPE EIGHT The Leader

TYPE TWO in balance gets the quality of TYPE FOUR The Individualist

58

Type ❸ The Performer

"That's why I started up a cycling club with a number of business friends. That's not only healthy, it's also fun and, more than anything, it's good for the business contacts. But sometimes at the end of a run I still want to sprint hard for a bit, because this boy may be nearly 50 now but he's still not pleased with second place. If I win it gives me a kick, that's all."

Mediator
9

8

1

Helper
2

7

6
Loyalist

3
Performer

5

4
Individualist

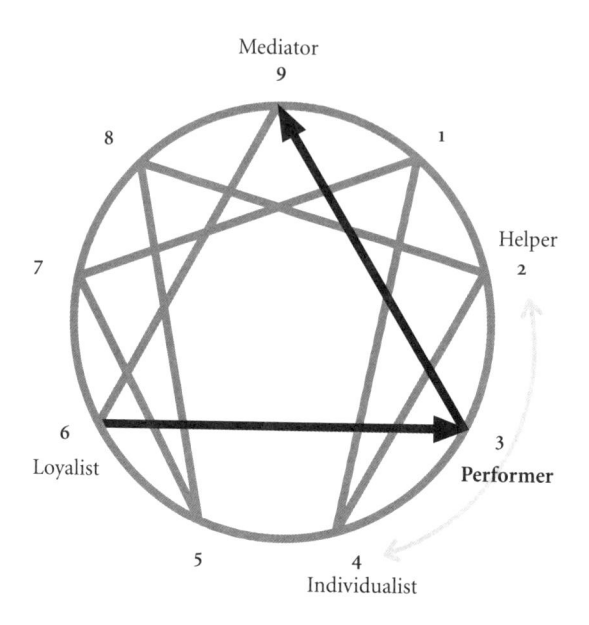

General description of a THREE
I like to be the best in what I do and it pleases me when I achieve something. I can do that because I work extremely hard on my success and attaining my goals. I hardly ever sit still and do nothing. I convert ideas quickly into action and am usually busy with a number of things at the same time. I can present myself well and I like it when people admire me. I make a self-assured impression; people sometimes find me arrogant. I dare to take risks and I work quickly and efficiently under time pressure. I find it annoying when others slow things down and hold me back.

Detailed description of a THREE
I am someone who likes to do things—someone who achieves things, scores successes. As a result I commit myself to something 100 per cent. Success is an important theme in my life. I would give almost everything for that. I don't know how to stop and can sometimes chase up others. In my single-mindedness I sometimes pass people over and ask too much of them. I have to take into account that others may reach their limit sooner. In order to have

success I am prepared to adapt myself and compromise. I know intuitively how to present myself positively in what I do or want to achieve. I find it important what others think of me and like it when people appreciate me. That is why I am sometimes tempted to present things as being better than they are or to play a role that makes a good impression on others. I often compare myself with others. If someone is good at something, then I want to be better at it. I like to win and find it irritating to lose. Actually I never really lose, because I sense where there is something to be won and where not.

No second place for me, please. I like competition and doing things efficiently. That is why I don't want to be hindered by anyone. I get a kick from attaining goals. It pleases me to be the centre of attention.

I am self-assured and not afraid to go after anything. A challenge is up my street. I like to work with clear objectives. I can present and sell myself well. Because of my self-confidence I can appear arrogant to people.

I find it very difficult to do nothing. I am always on the move, always busy. I am not good at knowing where my limits lie. Even when I am on holiday I fall into the trap of taking work with me. For me real relaxation is being alone; then I don't have to measure myself against anyone. But I can't be alone for long.

In my vision of life my viewpoint is that life is a competition and I can win by working hard and being successful. The most important values I stand for are performing well and professionalism. I am convinced that competition brings out the best in people.

I often ask myself such questions as: Do they appreciate me and do I get recognition and approval of my performance? My image of myself is: I am successful.

My primary motivation is that I want to be accepted for who I am. My secondary motives drive me:
- To gain acknowledgement and to create an attractive image of myself
- To gain attention and admiration and to make a good impression
- To maintain a harmonious relationship between myself and the outside world
- To prevent personal failures and to strive for success
- To book results and to improve myself
- To excel above others and to do that, or to use whatever is necessary to stay at the top.

My fear is that I am worthless and that I am not able to perform well. That is why I long to achieve something and feel worthy. I focus, therefore, on results, outcomes and competition. The colour that suits me best is yellow (noticeable, powerful, dynamic).

The Motivator appeals to me most as leadership style.

Core qualities of a THREE

Positive characteristics of mine are: efficient, self-confident, enthusiastic, competent and dynamic, diligent,

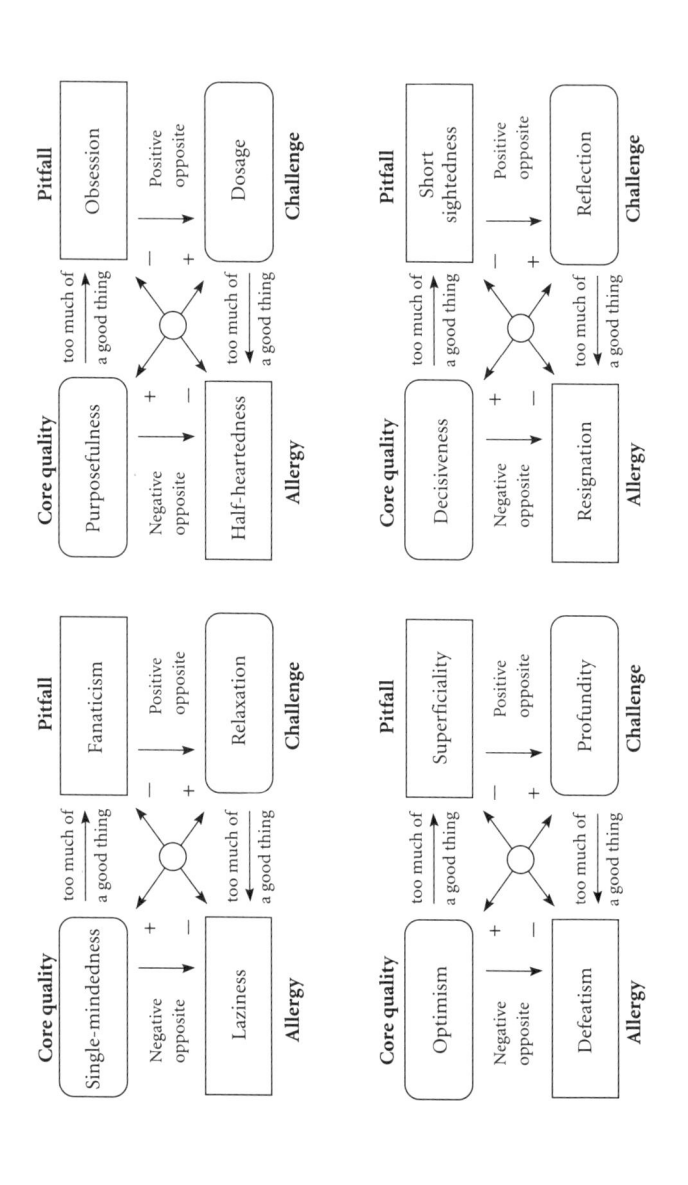

Core quality 1: Single-mindedness

	Pitfall
Core quality	Fanaticism
Single-mindedness	

- Negative opposite → Laziness (Allergy)
- Positive opposite → Relaxation (Challenge)
- too much of a good thing (both directions)

Core quality 2: Purposefulness

	Pitfall
Core quality	Obsession
Purposefulness	

- Negative opposite → Half-heartedness (Allergy)
- Positive opposite → Dosage (Challenge)
- too much of a good thing (both directions)

Core quality 3: Optimism

	Pitfall
Core quality	Superficiality
Optimism	

- Negative opposite → Defeatism (Allergy)
- Positive opposite → Profundity (Challenge)
- too much of a good thing (both directions)

Core quality 4: Decisiveness

	Pitfall
Core quality	Short sightedness
Decisiveness	

- Negative opposite → Resignation (Allergy)
- Positive opposite → Reflection (Challenge)
- too much of a good thing (both directions)

organised, purposeful, sure of myself, friendly, energetic, practical, resolute, persistent and capable, a motivator and team-builder. My core qualities are: single-mindedness, purposefulness, optimism and decisiveness

Less healthy aspects of a THREE

The less positive characteristics of a THREE are that he can be mechanical and calculating. He is allergic to inefficient behaviour and laziness. As a workaholic he tends, from his impatience, to negate feelings and sometimes even overshoots to being an intriguer. Under his performance impulse a certain tendency to deceit can be felt. In this respect he can appear to be like a chameleon and through this he acquires something fake.

You then ask yourself: Who is he really? What he wants to avoid are failures. Where he can be obsessive is in his desire to win every time. His defence mechanism is identification. That means that a THREE identifies himself completely with his professional role or his role in the group to which he belongs. This total absorption in the group or in the role prevents a THREE from being conscious of his unimportance and his failings.

When the Performer is under pressure and becomes stressed, he tends to display the less positive characteristics of the Mediator. He then abandons efficiency and can become passive and fall silent. Such characteristics as bitterness, self-aggression, apathy and egoism can come to the surface. The antidote that can help him most to break through well-worn patterns is honesty—honesty with himself, his true self under his roles.

Wings of a THREE

A Performer with a TWO wing is probably warmer, more sociable, more popular and more helpful than the Performer with a stronger FOUR wing. The Performer with a strong FOUR wing is more inward-looking, more sensitive, more artistic and richer in imagination.

A THREE *at his best*

What gives a Performer a feeling of fulfilment is obtaining recognition from others, being successful and radiating a good image to the outside world. When the Performer is relaxed and happy he has access to the positive characteristics of the Loyalist. He lays his mask aside and experiences his own identity, free from his roles. In his work he is loyal to himself and others instead of to his product. He is trustworthy and competent. This combination makes him a good leader. When he believes in something he learns to stick with it, even if it makes him unpopular. He learns to express his doubts and does not always have to be the best. A healthy Performer learns to work together with others, instead of competing with them and he develops trust that others can get things right.

At his best he inspires himself and his team members to perform well and be successful through taking initiatives, activating available sources, being efficient and persistent in achieving the desired results. His enthusiasm brings the team alive. He motivates others by complimenting them and highlighting their special talents. He balances his passion for achieving things with respect for the limitations of his workers.

A healthy THREE who has developed himself accepts his weak points, is faithful, loyal, honourable and just, sensitive and responsible. He has learned to gain access to his feelings and to integrate these in his dealings.

Core quadrants and arrow movements of a THREE

The relationships a THREE has with his arrow movements can be summarised in the following three core quadrants. (See figure on next page.)

Type Three

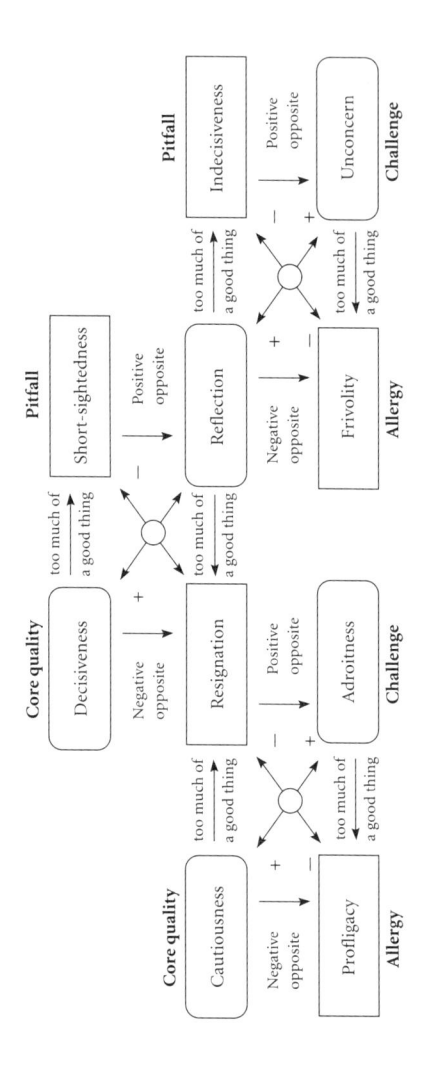

Core quality: Cautiousness
Negative opposite → Profligacy (**Allergy**)
+ / − too much of a good thing
Resignation (positive opposite: Adroitness — **Challenge**)

Core quality: Decisiveness
Negative opposite → Resignation
+ / − too much of a good thing
Reflection

Pitfall: Short-sightedness → Reflection
Negative opposite → Frivolity (**Allergy**)
too much of a good thing
Pitfall: Indecisiveness
Positive opposite → Unconcern (**Challenge**)

TYPE THREE under pressure
gets the pitfall of
TYPE NINE The Mediator

TYPE THREE in balance
gets the quality of
TYPE SIX The Loyalist

Type ❹ *The Individualist*

"Words soon degenerate into a succession of banalities and what for many is a good discussion is for me no more than listening to a series of vowels and consonants uttered by one or more persons. Perhaps it sounds a bit arrogant, but that's just how I experience it. I know I belong to a minority group in this. But I can't do anything else."

9
8
Perfectionist
1
Helper
2
7
Performer
3
6
5
Observer
4
Individualist

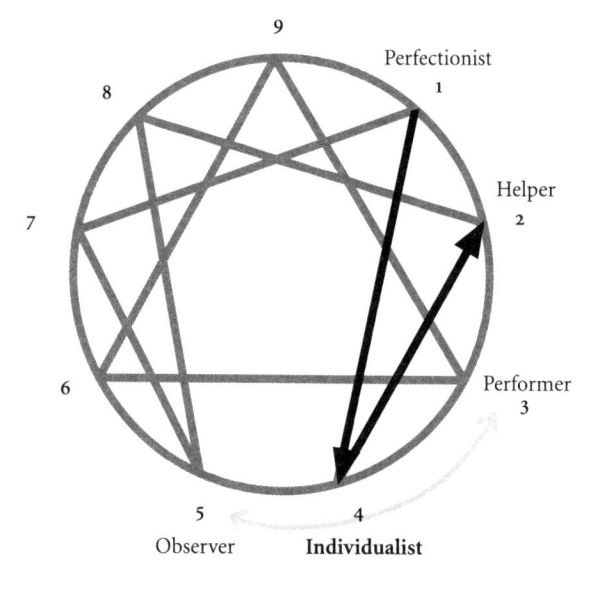

General description of a FOUR

I am a truly emotional person; I experience everything deeply and intensely. Others can call me over-dramatic on occasion from other people. I do not seem to belong. I like to do things differently, in my own way. I am unsystematic and I don't like routine and standard jobs.

I long for a deep relationship with someone else. I have searched for that my whole life long. It is always not quite right; something is missing. My life is marked by deep valleys and towering peaks. I need the depressions to experience the heights. Otherwise life is on an even keel and that is dull.

Detailed description of a FOUR

I am fond of a refined life-style, of the exceptional. I have a loathing for ordinary, everyday things. I have a tendency to look down a little on others who seem content with ordinary life. At the same time I envy those who are satisfied with a commonplace, easy life. I tend to feel myself something of an outsider who doesn't belong anywhere. Everyone who stands out as an exceptional personality can call up feelings of envy in me. Perhaps I feel that as a threat to my own exclusiveness.

Tragedy and romance are part of me. Everything I live through is out of proportion. Joy is rapture, sorrow is tragedy. Death and life occupy me a lot. I am always out to experience things deeply. That means that I am rather moody. From a great height, from feeling very good, I tumble down into a feeling of desolation. Actually—if I introduce myself to you—you should wonder what mood I am in.

I cling to the past and at the same time long for the future. Happiness is either something that has already been or something that is still to come, but is never attainable today. If I am down I can romanticise and idealise the past a great deal; when I am up I look to the future. I long for things which, once I have them, give me no satisfaction. Thus unrest and dissatisfaction, and feelings of unhappiness are always lying in wait.

I can exaggerate my emotions quite a lot. Often I feel that others do not understand me. Actually that is not so bad, because I am different anyway. I want to distinguish myself. On the other hand, I don't want to be different. It is a bit dualistic. I don't want to go with the crowd and I don't want to be an outsider. Solidarity with myself, contact with myself are important.

I am always looking for the perfect relationship. I want someone else to get to know me really well. I feel a strong attraction to the unattainable and the things that are not readily available. Relationships at a distance often seem to me to go better than being with someone day in day out. For me life is often a struggle. I don't find life easy and simple. I can long for things that will never happen. Occasionally there is some play-acting in my behaviour. I often see myself on the stage. Usually I perform for myself. I am constantly writing scripts and scenarios in my head. If I'm not careful a great part of my life will pass more in scripts that I perform for myself than in reality.

In my vision of life everything has to be authentic with depth and style. Even so there is something missing—I wish things were different! The most important values I stand for are authenticity and connection with people. My conviction is that organisations are human to the point where the individuality and feelings of people are respected.

I often ask myself such questions as: What is missing? The best is far off and not present; the negative is here and now, the positive is there and then. Why is it not as I imagined? Why is there disappointment again?

My image of myself is: I am different. My primary motivation is that I want to understand who I am. My secondary motives drive me:

- To stay in contact with my emotions and to express myself
- To create something beautiful as a means of communication with others
- To withdraw from others so that I can first deal with my emotions or face up to them

Diagram 1

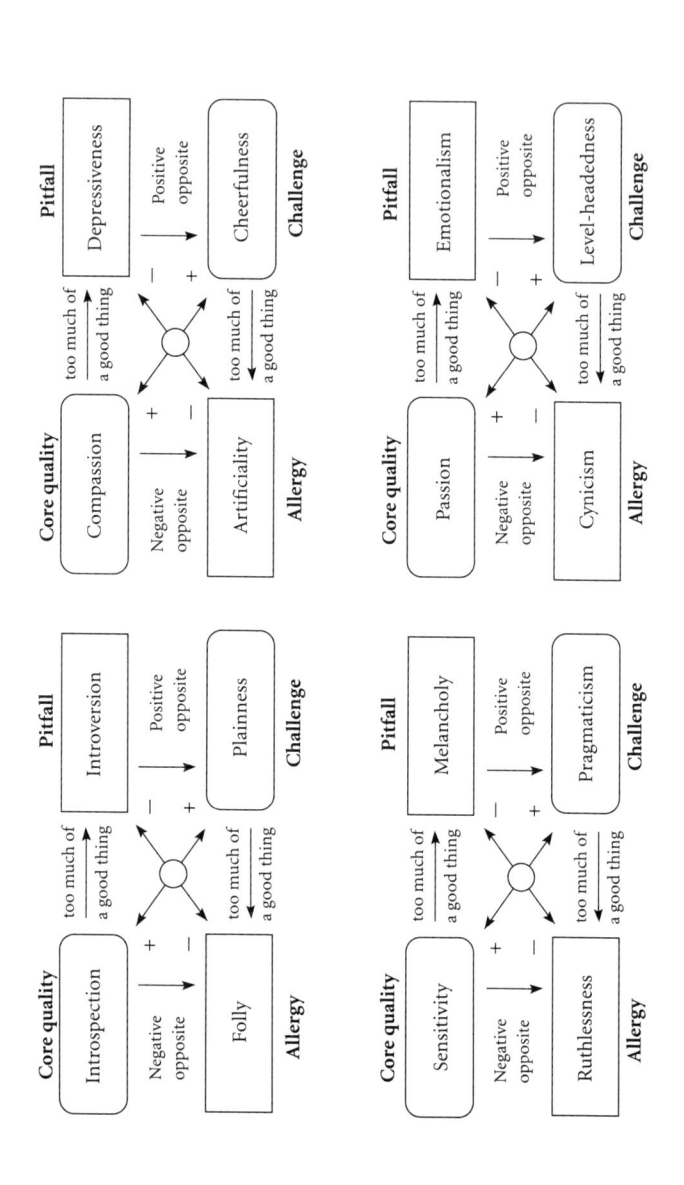

Core quality: Introspection
Pitfall: Introversion (too much of a good thing)
Allergy: Folly (negative opposite)
Challenge: Plainness (positive opposite of pitfall; too much of a good thing from allergy)

Diagram 2

Core quality: Compassion
Pitfall: Depressiveness
Allergy: Artificiality
Challenge: Cheerfulness

Diagram 3

Core quality: Sensitivity
Pitfall: Melancholy
Allergy: Ruthlessness
Challenge: Pragmatism

Diagram 4

Core quality: Passion
Pitfall: Emotionalism
Allergy: Cynicism
Challenge: Level-headedness

- To be able to handle my emotions or cope with them before I let myself in for something else
- To make good what I miss in the real world and to compensate for deficiency.

My fear is that I have no personal significance and that I am inadequate. Hence my deep longing to find myself and my identity and to feel significant. As a result I focus on the uniqueness of each person. The colour that suits me best is purple (changeable, melancholic, mystical, extraordinary).

Naturally the Individualist appeals to me most as leadership style.

No wonder that, apart from Individualist, they sometimes call me romantic, artist, writer or intuitivist.

Core qualities of a FOUR

Positive characteristics of mine are: sensitive, original, inventive, creative and involved. I am warm, intense and passionate, intuitive, artistic, refined, expressive, self-willed, visionary, good-natured, aesthetic and romantic. My core qualities are: introspection, compassion, sensitivity and passion.

Less healthy aspects of a FOUR

The less positive characteristics of a FOUR are that he can become emotionally unbalanced through changes of mood. He can then overshoot into deep depressions and high peaks, something that is difficult for others to understand.

He is allergic to disrespect and lack of feeling. From his 'being different' he has the tendency to become over-sensitive, to exaggerate and to dramatise. Sometimes he seeks too much attention and then feels misunderstood. His feeling that he is special can be interpreted as snobbism.

Under his individualism a certain tendency to envy can be felt. Why are others happy with ordinary things? From his feeling of 'being different' he avoids the every-day. Where he can be obsessive is in his melancholy and his focus on suffering. His defence mechanism is artistic sublimation. This defence mechanism ensures that feelings of inadequacy and vulnerability are not expressed directly. A FOUR expresses these feelings in an indirect way via symbols or he escapes into a romantic fantasy world. That prevents a FOUR from becoming conscious of daily reality and the dullness of his life.

The Individualist, when under pressure or stressed, tends to display the less positive characteristics of the Helper. He exchanges his inner world for recognition and appreciation by the world outside. He feels imprisoned, does what others want and cannot say 'no'. Feelings of self-pity and being a victim come to the surface. He gets the feeling that he is inadequate and can be pushy and start to manipulate with emotions. He can be complaining and withdraw himself. The antidote that can help him most to break through well-worn patterns is balance and stability.

Wings of a FOUR

The Individualist with a THREE wing is more ambitious, more aware of his image and more active in the outside world than a FOUR with a FIVE wing. The latter is more introverted, more intellectual, more reserved, more reflective.

A FOUR at his best

What gives an Individualist a sense of fulfilment is experiencing his own uniqueness by expressing his feelings. When the Individualist is relaxed and happy he has access to the positive characteristics of the Perfectionist. There a FOUR can transform his feelings of inferiority. He becomes more self-assured. In his work he approaches things in an active and solution-orientated manner. He has learned to reflect objectively on the solutions to problems without letting himself be carried away by emotions. A healthy FOUR focuses on one feeling at a time. What do I feel now and what can I do about it? He learns to keep to the facts, sees things in the proper proportion and does his work objectively. A healthy Individualist sets himself specific goals which he wants to attain. He follows clear standards and rules so that decisions will be made less impulsively.

At his best the Individualist is interested in his team members as individuals with unique talents. Being sensitive for what is personally important to his workers, he understands them intuitively. Workers feel they are heard. The work climate is human, with sensitivity. Unique in his leadership style, he is original in thinking up different ways of performing tasks and creating stylish products. Creativity and imagination are stimulated among the workers.

A healthy FOUR who has developed himself, is structured, orderly, disciplined, well-balanced, self-assured and responsible. He has learned to find satisfaction in being 'simply' happy.

Core quadrants and arrow movements of a FOUR

The relationships a FOUR has with his arrow movements can be summarised in the following three core quadrants.

Type Four

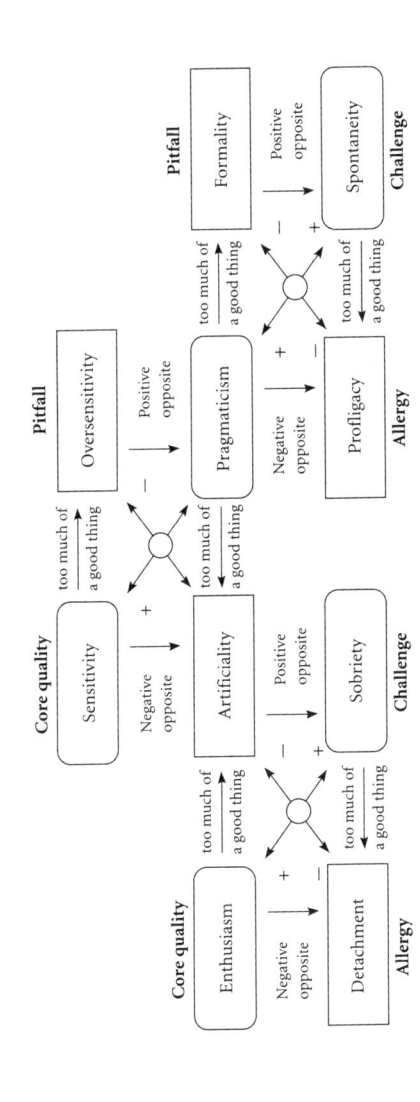

Core quality: Enthusiasm
Negative opposite → Detachment (**Allergy**)

Core quality: Sensitivity
Positive opposite: Artificiality
Negative opposite → Sobriety (**Challenge**)

Pitfall: Oversensitivity
Positive opposite: Pragmaticism
Negative opposite → Profligacy (**Allergy**)

Pitfall: Formality
Positive opposite → Spontaneity (**Challenge**)

(too much of a good thing connects Enthusiasm ↔ Artificiality, Sensitivity ↔ Detachment, Pragmaticism ↔ Formality, Oversensitivity ↔ Spontaneity)

Type four under pressure gets the pitfall of TYPE TWO The Helper

TYPE FOUR in balance gets the quality of TYPE ONE The Perfectionist

79

Type ⑤ The Observer

"Owls have always had a great attraction for me. I find them such unbelievably fascinating birds—that grace, that stoicism! It seems as if every act is thought through beforehand. In the last few months I have been busy identifying owl pellets, their so-called "plugs". This way you can obtain a precise picture of all the things an owl has eaten and everywhere he must have been."

Leader
8

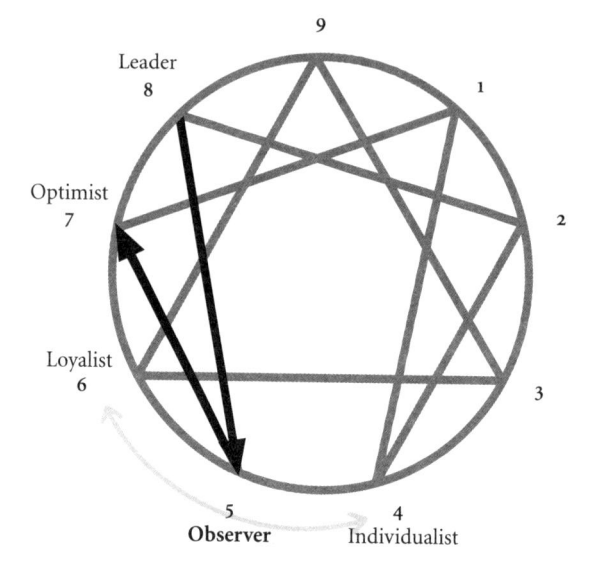

Optimist
7

Loyalist
6

5
Observer

4
Individualist

9

1

2

3

General description of a FIVE

I am a calm and analytical person. I save my time and energy and do not like it when people claim me or make too many demands on me. I prefer to observe rather than to join in something. I have a keen capacity for observation and a special feel for humour. I keep my distance emotionally and as a result often give an impression of aloofness. With emotional events it can sometimes be days later—when I am alone—before I experience my emotions. I attach great importance to my realm of thinking. I can concentrate well, make decisions easily and reason logically and objectively.

Detailed description of a FIVE

I withdraw easily and materially I can make do with little. I tend to believe that I can get a grip on life with knowledge and information. By understanding I obtain an overview and that gives me a feeling of safety, because knowing everything gives security. I like to be alone. Then I am not distracted. Only when I understand something can I act. That means that I think things over a lot. I like to observe from a distance and I cotton on to everything quickly. Then I withdraw—I need that in order to experience what has happened.

A lot of time for myself and privacy are important for keeping all the pieces together. If I am swamped I have to place the impressions in my frame of reference, otherwise I cannot act effectively. Naturally I want to keep enlarging my framework. Everything I am involved with has to fit within the frame. First think, then act. I often live inside my head. I store everything up and attempt to organise information. For me all the pieces must fit together. I am always looking for the key that enables me to understand.

I identify myself too much with what I know. From knowing I derive the meaning of my life. It irritates me when people cast doubt on my observations or insights. Then I think: if you could see what I see, then you would say I am right. Then I can appear arrogant. More often still I fall silent in such a situation and withdraw myself.

In a discussion I can listen very attentively and wait a long time before I take part in it. Then I miss the right moment and drag behind the discussion with my thoughts. It is sometimes difficult for others to keep a discussion going with me because I hate making small talk. If what is being said doesn't interest me, I sometimes notice that I am no longer present at all in the discussion.

I sometimes feel myself powerless and unimportant. In this I do not do myself and others justice. The feeling of standing alone and being an observer dates from much earlier. I react with detachment and seem to be able to cope alone. I am afraid that others will take me off guard, intrude on me, force me to do things. But I long very much for warmth and love.

I also deal with my body and emotions with detachment. I run the danger of not really experiencing my body. Usually I try not to display my emotions. That makes me vulnerable. I could lose control of them. Others could take me for an idiot. Nonetheless I actually have strong emotions that often come free later—if I'm at home and alone. Because I often withdraw or divide life up into boxes, I often experience an emptiness. It is difficult for me to ask others for something and to make it known that I need something. I try to do everything myself and alone.

In my vision of life my viewpoint is that I am master of my private world which is built on specialist knowledge. The most important values I stand for are autonomy and freedom. I am convinced that a vision gives an organisation direction and purpose.

I often ask myself such questions as: How does it fit together, what are the facts? What do others want of me? All my attention is directed towards observing, thinking and reducing feelings.

My image of myself is: I understand and realise the consequences. My primary motivation is that I want to understand the world around me. My secondary motives drive me:

Quadrant 1

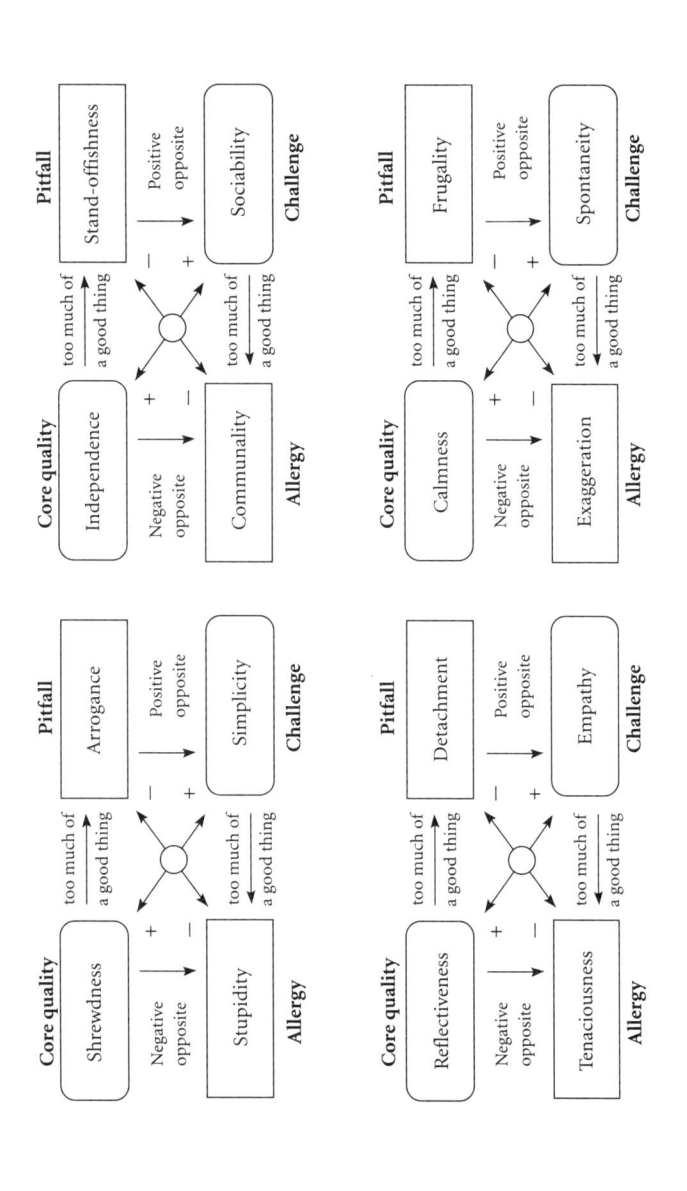

Core quality — Shrewdness
Pitfall — Arrogance
Allergy — Stupidity
Challenge — Simplicity

- Shrewdness → (Negative opposite) → Stupidity
- Arrogance → (Positive opposite) → Simplicity
- Shrewdness +/− Arrogance: too much of a good thing
- Simplicity +/− Stupidity: too much of a good thing

Quadrant 2

Core quality — Independence
Pitfall — Stand-offishness
Allergy — Communality
Challenge — Sociability

- Independence → (Negative opposite) → Communality
- Stand-offishness → (Positive opposite) → Sociability
- Independence +/− Stand-offishness: too much of a good thing
- Sociability +/− Communality: too much of a good thing

Quadrant 3

Core quality — Reflectiveness
Pitfall — Detachment
Allergy — Tenaciousness
Challenge — Empathy

- Reflectiveness → (Negative opposite) → Tenaciousness
- Detachment → (Positive opposite) → Empathy
- Reflectiveness +/− Detachment: too much of a good thing
- Empathy +/− Tenaciousness: too much of a good thing

Quadrant 4

Core quality — Calmness
Pitfall — Frugality
Allergy — Exaggeration
Challenge — Spontaneity

- Calmness → (Negative opposite) → Exaggeration
- Frugality → (Positive opposite) → Spontaneity
- Calmness +/− Frugality: too much of a good thing
- Spontaneity +/− Exaggeration: too much of a good thing

- To know everything with certainty and to avoid emptiness or ignorance
- To understand everything and to observe
- To have intellectual certainty and to interpret everything according to or in line with an associative/unifying idea
- To discard that which does not accord with my own ideas
- To isolate myself from everything that seems to threaten me.

My fear is emptiness, not being able to think and being incompetent. For me the tenet *cogito ergo sum* (I think, therefore I am) applies strongly. That is why I have developed my thinking and my competency by acquiring knowledge. As a result I focus on rational structures and critical thought. The colour that suits me best is blue (introvert, restful, detached).

My favourite leadership style is the System-maker.

No wonder that they sometimes call me observer, thinker, researcher or philosopher.

Core qualities of a FIVE

Positive characteristics of mine are: understanding, clear, philosophic and bright. I am logical, objective, succinct, analytical and thirsty for knowledge. My core qualities are: shrewdness, independence, reflectiveness and calmness.

Less healthy aspects of a FIVE

The less positive characteristics of a FIVE are that he can be soloistic, chilly, cold and stingy with time and energy. Then he is afraid of feelings, becomes abstract, postpones matters and avoids commitment. He is allergic to irrational behaviour and emotional reactions. He is often socially clumsy and uninvolved. Avarice can sometimes be felt under his shrewdness and calmness. What he avoids is emptiness in his head, not being able to think and understand. Where he can be obsessive is in separating himself and shutting himself up in his ivory tower. His defence mechanism is isolation. He withdraws himself into his world of thoughts to organise reality for himself and free himself from his emotions. This prevents a FIVE from becoming conscious of his fear of not knowing enough.

When the Observer is under pressure he tends to display the less positive characteristics of the Optimist. He can then let go of reality and sail off in a sea of daydreaming and aimless activity. At that stage he loses overall sight of things, something that can lead to nervous acts, superficiality, untrustworthiness, irrealistic and irresponsible behaviour. The antidote that can help him most to break through well-worn patterns is objectivity and unattachment.

Wings of a FIVE

An Observer with a developed FOUR wing is more creative, more sensitive, more orientated towards people and has a greater empathy. An Observer with a strong SIX wing is more loyal, careful and sceptical.

A FIVE at his best

What gives a FIVE a sense of fulfilment is having insight and, based on that, his personally founded judgement, and being able to see through and understand things. When relaxed the Observer has access to the positive characteristics of the Leader. Decisiveness and self-confidence characterise the FIVE who moves towards the EIGHT: he makes himself manifest in the outside world, puts knowledge into practice and goes after things. He has power of conviction and is influential. He experiences feelings of personal power, is more assertive and more at his ease with people.

In his work he can change things and influence situations. He is in contact with his inner authority and goes for the things in which he believes. He can say to himself: I am powerful, I can act. He has the power to go against the current and can say what he does and doesn't want. He learns to listen to the language of his body, his intuition, his heart and his emotions. He can also define limits himself instead of withdrawing himself.

At his best he is in contact with his personal power and invites team members to exchange ideas about projects with each other. With his overall view he can easily plan long-term projects. Untangling complex affairs into simple elements and analysing them enables him to obtain clear solutions to problems. Responsibility is delegated to team members to enable them to perform their tasks in their own way. He dares to risk converting his ideas into actions and to share his vision with others so that he can profit from their insight.

A healthy FIVE who has developed himself has learned to participate and be emotionally involved with people.

Core quadrants and arrow movements of a FIVE

The relationships a FIVE has with his arrow movements can be summarised in the following three core quadrants.

Type Five

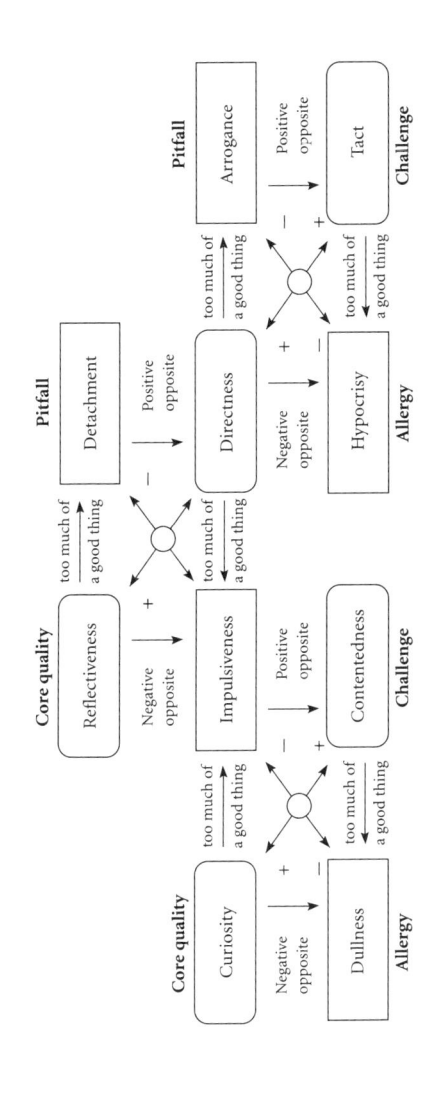

Core quality: Reflectiveness → (Negative opposite) Impulsiveness **Pitfall:** Detachment → (Positive opposite) Directness

Reflectiveness + Directness (too much of a good thing both ways) −

Detachment — Positive opposite → Directness

Directness → Positive opposite → Contentedness **Challenge**
Impulsiveness → Negative opposite → Hypocrisy **Allergy**

Pitfall: Arrogance → Positive opposite → Tact **Challenge**

Directness + / − Arrogance (too much of a good thing)

Core quality: Curiosity → (Negative opposite) Dullness **Allergy**

Curiosity + Impulsiveness (too much of a good thing) −

Type five under pressure gets the pitfall of type seven The Optimist

Type five in balance gets the quality of type eight The Leader

Type ❻ The Loyalist

"Yes, I'm a deep one. I love my work and I believe that my colleagues value me, but naturally you can never be completely sure of that.

"I have developed a kind of sixth sense for everything that can contain danger. I am, as it were, constantly prepared for everything that can go wrong. I have to say honestly that that can sometimes be a hindrance, I mean that pondering and weighing things up."

Mediator
9

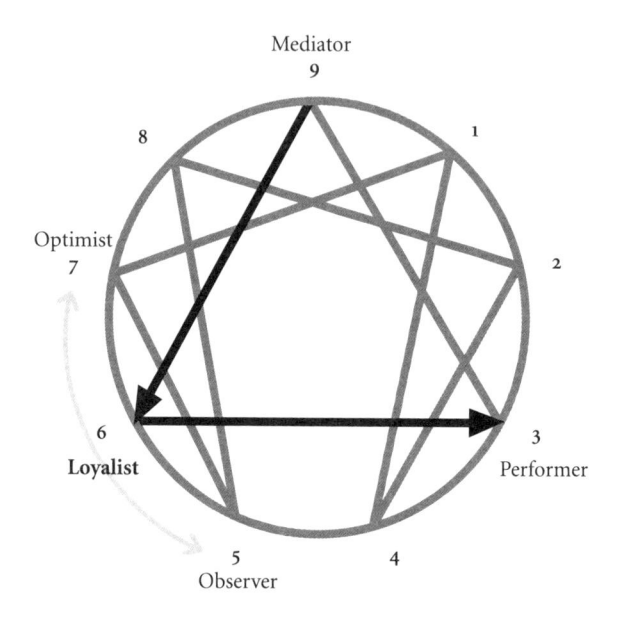

8   1

Optimist
7

                2

6   3
Loyalist   Performer

       5   4
    Observer

General description of a SIX

I have a lively imagination, particularly where things that can go wrong are concerned. I presume that things will go amiss so that I can in any event be prepared. I doubt a lot and it can take a while before I make a decision. I can therefore extend things a long way before me. I have a kind of sixth sense for detecting or sensing danger. I have difficulty with unexpected things that make my safety and certainty unsteady. My sense of duty is strong and if I commit myself to something or someone then I am very loyal. I sometimes tend to be too serious and to take things literally. When someone criticises me I feel under attack. That makes me uncertain. I like belonging to a group—that gives me a feeling of safety.

Detailed description of a SIX

I am blessed with a very powerful imagination. Being strongly orientated towards everything that could involve danger, I have a certain dread of success.

Fear for danger is, as it were, in my blood. Even in a situation that is, in general, favourable, I tend to turn my attention to a negative detail and magnify it. Without knowing it I keep asking questions like: What must I watch out for? Do they really mean what they say? Life is full of threats and I constantly have the feeling that I have to be prepared for ill intentions. I distrust everyone until there is proof to the contrary. I am always careful. I feel the tension of anxiety in my body. Even though it is difficult for me to live with that anxiety, fearful apprehension is still for me something familiar and it offers me a kind of safety. I am, as it were, thoroughly prepared for everything that can happen to me.

Thus I often have a great many questions. You will regularly hear me use the words 'yes, but…'. It costs me a good deal of energy not to keep asking questions, to become numb. Part of my fear arises from my rich imagination about all the things that can happen and go wrong. If I have a plan or an idea, fear and doubt come on the scene immediately. That has a paralysing effect. Sometimes I break through my fear and then I miss no opportunity. I can then act very impulsively and take a leap in the dark. I do not recognise myself then. My fear goes hand in hand with doubts, first and foremost about myself. That is why I can be so indecisive and making a decision costs me effort. I often wait too long; hundreds of things are going through my head.

Traditions and rules are important for me. People can let you down, but traditions and laws not. They make things clear. Trusting and being loyal play a major role in my life. What you promise, you have to do. I am loyal to people I trust, through thick and thin. I like to be with like-minded people—that gives me a safe feeling. But they have to use a quiet approach with me. It is important for me to know what others expect of me. Goals, guidelines—I like to know where I stand. Taking things literally is also something that suits me. I have a kind of transmitter inside me that I use to sound out the surroundings for danger. I often have ambivalent feelings and I actually feel them both at the same time. I often feel tense, feel very much shut up in my head. I can listen well and sense the intentions of others. Nonetheless, because of my doubts, I don't really listen to my intuition.

In my vision of life my viewpoint is that the world is dangerous, the truth lies hidden and things are not as they seem. The most important values I stand for are safety and openness. I am convinced that organisations have to offer a feeling of unity. I often ask myself such questions as: Is what they are saying right? For whom or for what must I watch out? All my attention is directed to possible danger and hidden meanings.

My image of myself is: I do my duty and behave well. My primary motivation is to be secure and safe.

My secondary motives drive me:
- To belong to a group in order to secure approval and safety
- To be regarded as friendly and to win acceptance
- To test for myself the attitudes and opinions of others
- To make myself count in order to overcome my fear

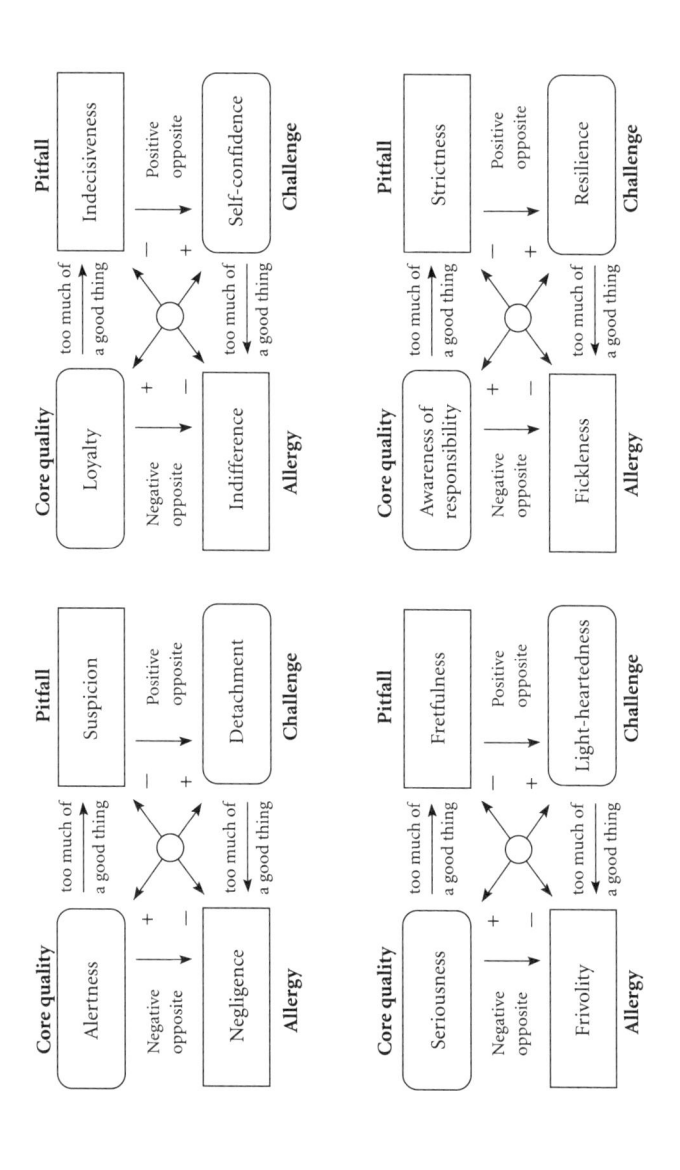

Core quality	**Pitfall**
Alertness	Suspicion

Alertness → Negligence (Negative opposite)
Suspicion → Detachment (Positive opposite)

too much of a good thing / too much of a good thing

Allergy: Negligence — **Challenge**: Detachment

Core quality	**Pitfall**
Loyalty	Indecisiveness

Loyalty → Indifference (Negative opposite)
Indecisiveness → Self-confidence (Positive opposite)

Allergy: Indifference — **Challenge**: Self-confidence

Core quality	**Pitfall**
Seriousness	Fretfulness

Seriousness → Frivolity (Negative opposite)
Fretfulness → Light-heartedness (Positive opposite)

Allergy: Frivolity — **Challenge**: Light-heartedness

Core quality	**Pitfall**
Awareness of responsibility	Strictness

Awareness of responsibility → Fickleness (Negative opposite)
Strictness → Resilience (Positive opposite)

Allergy: Fickleness — **Challenge**: Resilience

- To be reassured if I am afraid, to recover my security and to let the person with authority help me.

My fear is that I am alone and unable to survive. My desire is to belong somewhere, to have support. I would rather be alone than lonely. I focus primarily on human relationships and commitment. The colour that suits me best is beige (adaptable, richly variegated, mixed).

My favourite leadership style is the Team-player.

No wonder that they also call me sometimes the devil's advocate, doubter or waiter.

Core qualities of a six

Positive characteristics of mine are: trustworthy, respectful, honourable, resolute and loyal. I am stabilising, judicious, tenacious, watchful and fair. My core qualities are: alertness, loyalty, seriousness and awareness of responsibility.

Less healthy aspects of a six

The less positive characteristics of a six are that he can be dogmatic, suspicious, uncompromising and inclined to be defeatist. He is also sometimes timid, doubtful, conservative and unsure. He is allergic to untrustworthiness and ambiguity. Fear can be felt quite often under his loyalty. What he avoids is improper behaviour, because that can mean the disapproval of others. What he can be obsessive in is watching for danger. His most important defence mechanism is projection. What he doesn't want to see in himself, he lays at the door of another. By projecting negative feelings on other people a SIX prevents himself from being conscious of his own uncertainty.

The Loyalist under pressure has the tendency to display the less positive characteristics of the Performer. His behaviour is restless and he becomes calculating and even more suspicious of someone's motives. He can become aggressive and authoritarian. Lack of feeling and a mechanical zest for work can also come to the surface. The antidote that can help him most to break through well-worn patterns is courage.

Wings of a SIX

If a Loyalist has a FIVE wing stronger than a SEVEN wing then he tends to be more detached, more conservative, more introverted and more intellectual. If the SEVEN wing is more dominant then he is more extrovert, more active, more materialistic and more impulsive. He can put things in perspective easier and have pleasure.

A SIX at his best

It gives a Loyalist a sense of fulfilment if he satisfies expectations and has a feeling of solidarity. When relaxed the Loyalist has access to the positive characteristics of the Mediator. He radiates peace and quiet, relaxation, harmony, airiness and trust. By slowing down he can get things in perspective better and learn to concentrate on himself instead of being subject to the authority outside himself. In addition he can become more conscious of bodily sensations and develop a large degree of empathy. In his work he has developed inner power and self-confidence. He has learned to trust in his own capabilities and stand behind his vision. He has also learned to deal with his negative thinking. By using his questions and doubts positively, he can become enthusiastic about all possibly good results.

He learns to be peaceful and quiet within himself and realises that solutions and answers lie in himself. He takes the time to let answers come to the surface themselves. Daring to go with the current and relaxing in the process give him confidence and security. He realises that going against the current and fighting are not always the solutions.

At his best a six sees himself as part of a team with whose ideas he wants to identify himself. Workers are encouraged to feel themselves a part of the team and to think about common goals. Committed to the common aim of the organisation, he places the well-being of the team above individual interests. Loyalty, trustworthiness and hard work are rewarded so that problems are solved together.

A healthy six has learned to trust himself and others.

Core quadrants and arrow movements of a six
The relationships a six has with his arrow movements can be summarised in the following three core quadrants. (See figure on next page.)

Type Six

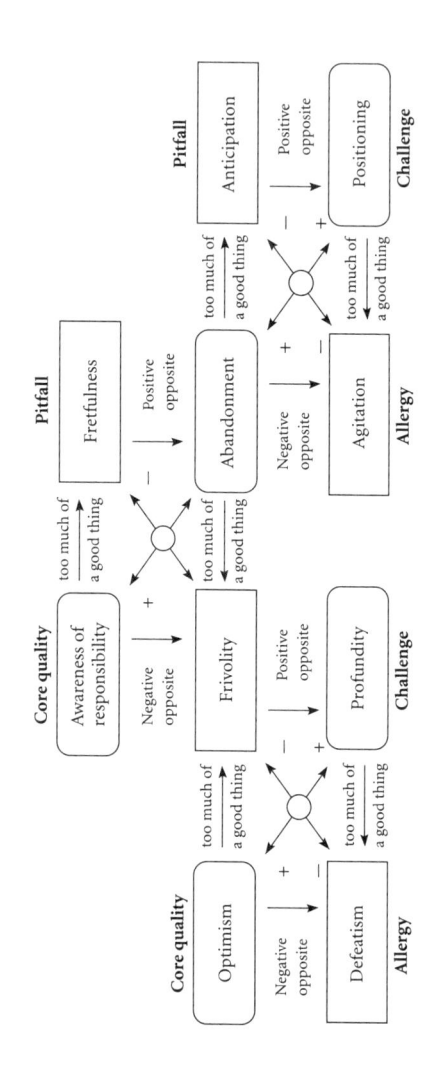

Core quality: Awareness of responsibility
Pitfall: Fretfulness (Positive opposite of Awareness of responsibility via Abandonment)
Allergy: Agitation
Challenge: Profundity

Core quality: Optimism
Allergy: Defeatism

Pitfall: Anticipation
Challenge: Positioning

Frivolity — Positive opposite → Profundity
Awareness of responsibility — Negative opposite → Frivolity
Optimism — Negative opposite → Defeatism
Abandonment — Negative opposite → Agitation
Fretfulness — Positive opposite → Abandonment
Anticipation — Positive opposite → Positioning

too much of a good thing / too much of a good thing

TYPE SIX under pressure gets the pitfall of
TYPE THREE The Performer

TYPE SIX in balance gets the quality of
TYPE NINE The Mediator

Type ❼ The Optimist

"Do I dare sometimes to pick out the plums in life for myself? Sure, why not? Perhaps I'm an odd character, but you just have to take me as I am. Our good Lord didn't give us a nose and tastebuds for nothing. So use them then. There's so much to discover, but naturally you have to be open for it. I've never yet been bored with myself. I'm full to the brim with plans. I'm always looking for new challenges."

Leader
8

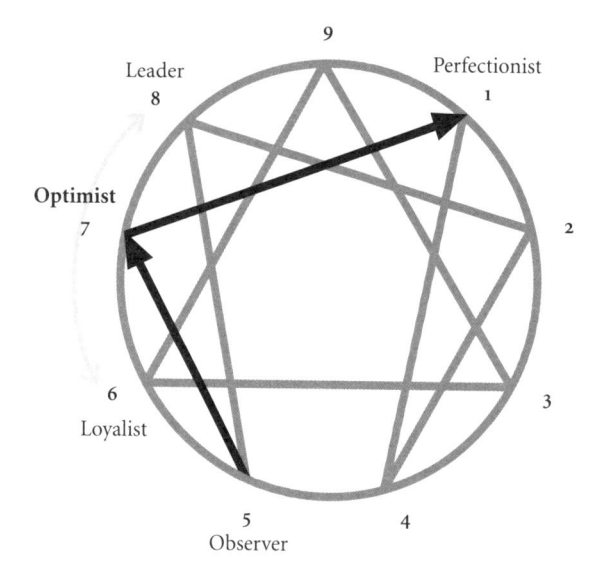

Perfectionist
1

Optimist
7

2

6
Loyalist

3

5
Observer

4

9

General description of a SEVEN

By nature I am an optimist; I see the sunny side of everything and enjoy life. I have a very active mind that jumps quickly back and forth from one idea to another. I am cheerful as long as I can do what I want and I am always open to new ideas. I do not bind myself easily, because I don't like to limit myself. It is important for me to have a large number of options.

I steer clear of pain as far as possible. When I no longer find something pleasant, it is difficult for me to keep my attention on it. I would rather think about something new. I usually say what I think and that can occasionally get me into difficulties. I am a generaliser and like to bundle ideas and information into one whole.

Detailed description of a SEVEN

I take pleasure in everything and want to enjoy life. I like to watch how people interact with one another. I try to discover the good in everything. By nature I am optimistic, cheerful and vivacious. I have the feeling that everything is possible in life. There are always new choices and possibilities. I don't like to be pinned down to something. Commitment is difficult for me. If I commit myself I have to give up my sense of an unlimited future. I am hungry for new experiences. I run the danger of closing my eyes to the painful aspects of life. One of the ways to bypass them is via my passion for making plans.

Everything is possible in my mind. I am not so good at converting my plans into deeds. I start things, but do not always finish them. I do many things at the same time and intermingled. Even so I keep the overview. I have a great many hobbies. I have the tendency to hop from one thing to the other and in this respect I remain a bit superficial.

I find that everything should be pleasant. Why should you be sombre? Life is one big party. I give a positive twist to everything. I want to avoid as much as possible what is painful and heavy. I like to keep things light. I don't know what to do about people in trouble. In the first instance I will try to cheer them up and help them, because I don't want them to experience difficulties. I think it is just fine if everybody is happy. I find pain unpleasant and I would really like to sail round it for others as well. I can tell stories with the best of them and I enjoy word-play. I am something of an artist with words and can often use them to get my way.

In my vision of life my viewpoint is that the world is full of exciting possibilities, concepts and experiences. It is my mission to explore these.

The most important values I stand for are adventure and

pleasure. I am convinced that optimism and enthusiasm within an organisation are driving forces. I often ask myself such questions as: Is it pleasant here? What is there to be experienced? All my attention is directed to action, excitement, positive future possibilities, options and putting information in perspective. My image of myself is: I am happy. My primary motivation is that I want to be glad, happy and content. My secondary motives drive me:

- To avoid pain, discomfort and fear
- To amuse myself and have pleasure
- Not to put restrictions on myself
- To get what I want
- To repress fear by keeping busy
- To give way to impulses and to flee from fear.

My fear is that I am being deprived or missing out. That is probably the reason for my desire to experience as much as possible and so attain completeness. In any event I don't want to miss anything nice. That is why I focus on satisfaction and innovation. The colour that suits me is green (vital, joyful and luxuriant).

My favourite leadership style is the Applauder.

No wonder that they sometimes also call me the hedonist, generaliser, adventurer or dreamer.

Core qualities of a SEVEN
Positive characteristics of mine are that I am optimistic, creative, enthusiastic, vivacious, inventive, exciting, enter-

Diagram 1

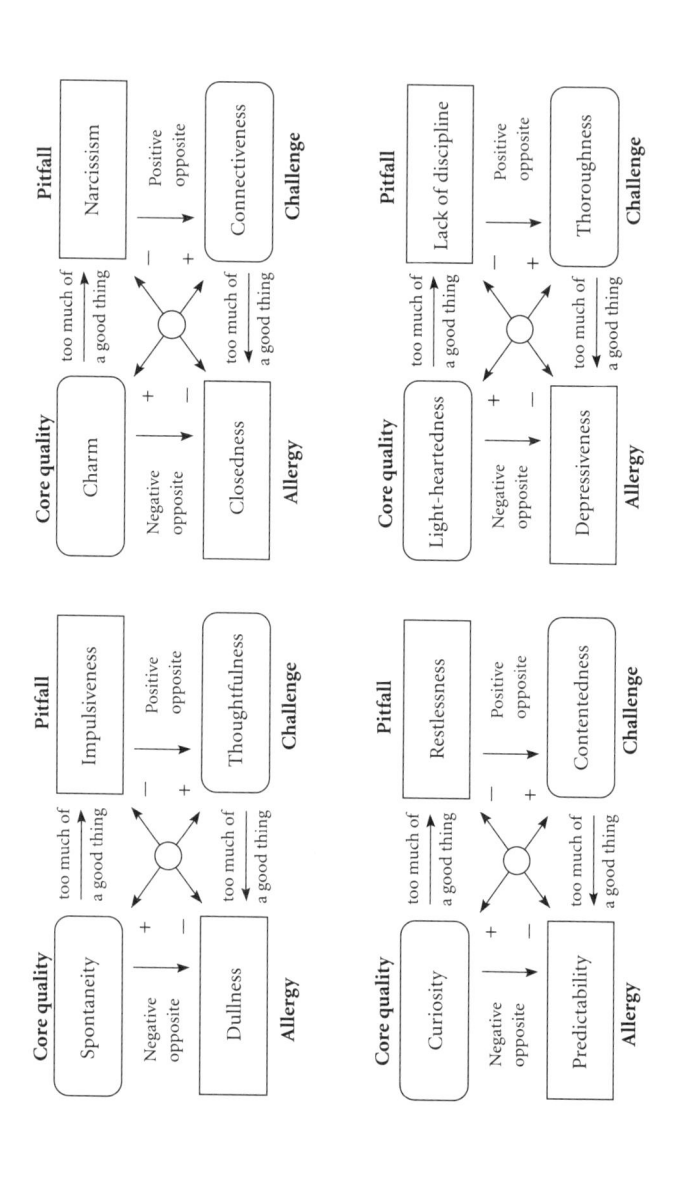

Core quality: Spontaneity
Pitfall: Impulsiveness
Allergy: Dullness
Challenge: Thoughtfulness

- Spontaneity — (+) — too much of a good thing → Impulsiveness
- Impulsiveness — Positive opposite → Thoughtfulness
- Spontaneity — Negative opposite → Dullness
- Dullness — (−/+) too much of a good thing → Thoughtfulness

Diagram 2

Core quality: Charm
Pitfall: Narcissism
Allergy: Closedness
Challenge: Connectiveness

- Charm — (+) — too much of a good thing → Narcissism
- Narcissism — Positive opposite → Connectiveness
- Charm — Negative opposite → Closedness
- Closedness — too much of a good thing → Connectiveness

Diagram 3

Core quality: Curiosity
Pitfall: Restlessness
Allergy: Predictability
Challenge: Contentedness

- Curiosity — (+) — too much of a good thing → Restlessness
- Restlessness — Positive opposite → Contentedness
- Curiosity — Negative opposite → Predictability
- Predictability — too much of a good thing → Contentedness

Diagram 4

Core quality: Light-heartedness
Pitfall: Lack of discipline
Allergy: Depressiveness
Challenge: Thoroughness

- Light-heartedness — (+) — too much of a good thing → Lack of discipline
- Lack of discipline — Positive opposite → Thoroughness
- Light-heartedness — Negative opposite → Depressiveness
- Depressiveness — too much of a good thing → Thoroughness

taining, stimulating, clever and zestful. My core qualities are: spontaneity, charm, curiosity and light-heartedness.

Less healthy aspects of a SEVEN

The less positive characteristics of a SEVEN are that he is superficial, easily distracted, impulsive, muddled and daydreamy; sometimes also irresponsible, unreliable, unrealistic or even narcissistic. He is allergic to complaining and being limited. Immoderation can occasionally be felt under his optimism. What he avoids is pain and where he can be obsessive is in thinking he is genial. His defence mechanism is rationalisation. That means that he gives to everything another—a positive—meaning. In this way a SEVEN prevents himself from being conscious of his pain.

The Optimist under pressure or stress tends to display the less positive characteristics of the Perfectionist. Noticeable changes in behaviour can be that he becomes cynical and starts to focus on imperfection. That can make him a critical, intolerant slave-driver who is inflexible, demanding and angry. The antidote that can help him most to break through worn-out patterns is sobriety.

Wings of a SEVEN

If the SIX wing is more dominant in an Optimist, then he is more loyal, more engaging, more responsible and more conservative, because he worries a little more. A stronger EIGHT influence makes an Optimist more exuberant, more decisive, more aggressive, more achievement-orientated, more impulsive and more aimed at pleasure.

A SEVEN at his best

What gives an Optimist a feeling of fulfilment is making pleasant plans for the future. When relaxed the Optimist has access to the positive characteristics of the Observer. He is able to stick to one or two things, to limit himself. He can take the time in peace and quiet to experience a deeper involvement with people and ideas. Other possible changes are that he develops more austerity and profundity. He becomes more philosophic, more curious, more discerning and he observes more. That leads to less fragmentation and more detachment for assimilating experiences.

In his work he has learned to temper a little his enthusiasm for an excessive number of projects. He concentrates on fewer tasks at the same time. He learns to face unpleasant matters and handle them better as a result. He balances his creative and intuitive mind by taking practical and realistic steps to round off projects. A SEVEN can come up with everything there is: the good and the bad, the pleasure and the pain. He does what is worthwhile. He learns to stay in the here and now and to resist his need to see himself in a pleasant future. He does what he does, instead of day-dreaming. Situations are not beautified when he faces reality and he learns to express his anger.

At his best the Optimist stimulates his team members

to be enthusiastic about their work. Even though a SEVEN hates confrontations and the forcing of decisions, he can work well with team members who are different. The optimism of the SEVEN creates a positive atmosphere and his inspiration in seeing the positive sides of challenging tasks peps up morale. His search for new ideas and alternative methods stimulates workers to adopt innovative strategies and adapt themselves to different circumstances.

A healthy SEVEN has learned to stick to one thing and commit himself.

Core quadrants and arrow movements of a SEVEN

The relationships a SEVEN has with his arrow movements can be summarised in the following three core quadrants. (See figure on next page.)

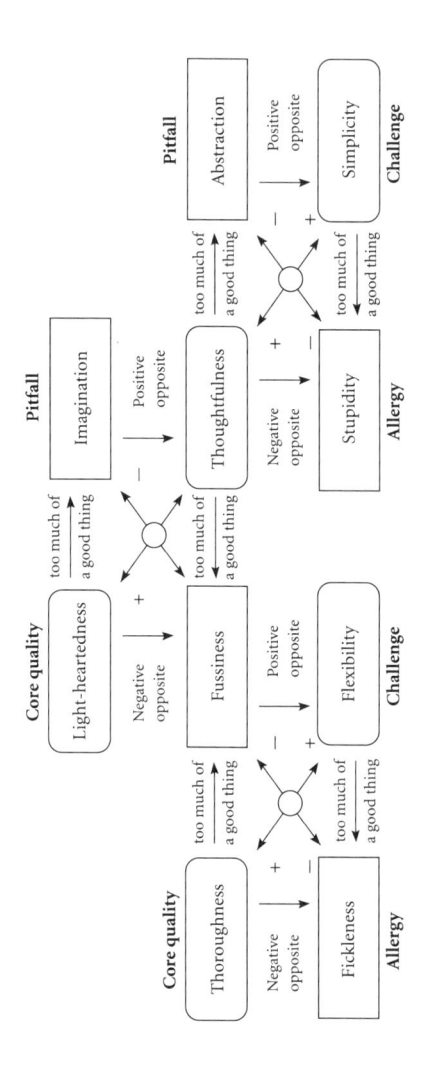

Type Seven

Core quality: Light-heartedness → (+) Fussiness → (Positive opposite) Flexibility — **Challenge**
Light-heartedness (Negative opposite) → Stupidity

Pitfall: Imagination → (Positive opposite) Thoughtfulness → (Negative opposite) Stupidity — **Allergy**

Core quality: Thoroughness → (+) Fickleness — **Allergy**
Thoroughness (Negative opposite) → Fickleness

Pitfall: Abstraction → (Positive opposite) Simplicity — **Challenge**

Arrows labeled "too much of a good thing" connect the core qualities to their pitfalls and the challenges to the allergies.

TYPE SEVEN under pressure gets the pitfall of TYPE ONE The Perfectionist

TYPE SEVEN in balance gets the quality of TYPE FIVE The Observer

Type ❽ The Leader

"I'm strong, but fair. There are only a few people who really know me, and those people know how to value me. I sometimes appear hard. But let me say first that there's no one harder on himself than I am.

"If decisions have to be made, knots have to be cut through and then you have to dare to be hard. Soft surgeons leave stinking wounds."

Mediator
9

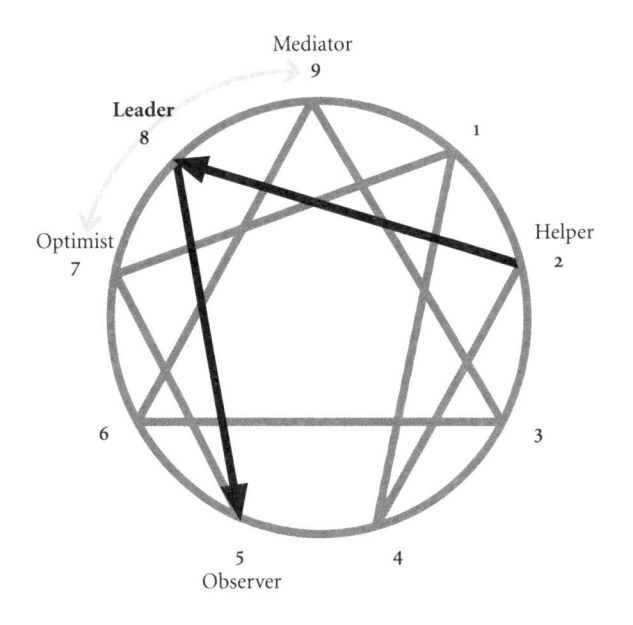

Leader
8

Helper
2

Optimist
7

6

3

5
Observer

4

General description of an EIGHT

I am energetic and geared to action. I have an all-or-nothing approach to things. I find it important to be strong, honest and trustworthy. Because of my clarity you know what you have in me. I trust hardly anyone. The few people I trust have proved that they are worth that trust. I have difficulty with people who prevaricate; I sense it when someone is a fake and I don't sweep that under the carpet. I love excitement and challenge. I don't like taking orders, and not at all from people I don't respect. I would rather follow my own wishes and keep the reins in my own hands. I am easily angered and show it immediately. Then I am rid of it quickly again. I can't stand injustice. When I see somebody treating someone weaker unjustly, then I back up the weaker person.

Detailed description of an EIGHT

I am strong and can do everything. I am afraid of nothing, certainly not if I compare myself with others. I see it as a challenge to show that I can manage things alone. I value independence highly. I enjoy confrontation. I am a fighter;

I never give in. At the same time I am not very sensitive in my dealings. My use of words is definitely not polished. If I have doubts I don't show them. I don't allow others to rule me. Power and control play a major role in my life: I like to be the boss. If I feel that someone is stronger or has more power than I have, I want to match forces with him. But you should realise that under my strong, hard exterior lies a soft vulnerable core. A little child lives in me that longs for tenderness. But I dare to let the soft side be seen by only a few people. With children I feel at ease.

I stand up for truth and justice. I tend to blame others if something goes wrong. Convinced that I am right, I can sweep the opinions of others off the table. I have a strong feeling for justice, but I readily take the reins in my own hands. Then there can be a narrowing of understanding. My truth then becomes the only truth. What others say or mean I label as nonsense. I can easily act as my own judge and jury and decide who is good and who bad, who should be rewarded and who punished. Moreover I have the tendency not to interpret rules and regulations so precisely. I make those myself. But here too I am a harsh judge on myself if I have been in the wrong.

Friendship means a lot to me. I invest a great deal in it. I am not easy because I ask a lot. I am not generous or casual in apportioning affection. I can't bear people who cling to me; I feel uncomfortable with them.

I react immediately and wholly by instinct. I can jump in somewhere without thinking. Then I follow my feelings.

I express something just the way I feel it and experience it. I also have difficulty with people who are afraid to be open. If I'm not careful my remarks make them withdraw farther into their shells.

I am a passionate person. That is apparent from the way I talk about people and things. My whole body is involved. You can see in my body what I feel. I approach others with intensity, power of conviction and energy. They can get the feeling that I don't give them any space.

I have a great deal of energy—more than most, I've discovered. If I am busy with something or amusing myself, then I do not know how to stop. I head straight for my goal. You know with me exactly where I stand. I am looking for my place within the whole. I like to test people to see how they react. People have to indicate their limits themselves and say 'stop'.

I sense where people's weak spots are. Naturally I try to draw them out in order to prompt their reactions. I take the lead if no one else does. I like giving orders. I go all out for something however awkward a situation is. I respect power in others. I love challenges. Being old and sick is troublesome, for then I am dependent. I don't allow that. Actually I have a very small heart; if you touch that, you may do almost anything.

I can easily let myself be dragged along by my emotions and hurt those that I love most. But you should know that I can be very angry with and hard on myself. If an injustice is done to me, I go immediately into action to do something about it. Taking revenge is putting it a little too strongly, but it can come close to it.

I can feel very restless within myself; I need space. If I am not pleasantly occupied with something, I also become restless. Then I get bored. My energy and restlessness make me immoderate: too much, too long, too late. Daring to give in—that is the way I must go, not having constantly to win and be the strong one. A close, intimate relationship can open my heart and let the soft, vulnerable side come to the surface. Then I learn that surrendering does not mean losing.

In my vision of life my viewpoint is that the world is unjust. I defend the weak, unmask impostors and expose injustice. The most important values I stand for are independence and influence.

I am convinced that authority and power are the most important motive forces within an organisation. I often ask myself such questions as: Who or what forms a threat for me? Where does the power lie? All my attention is directed to power, domination and possible loss of control.

My image of myself is: I am strong. My primary motivation is that I am full of confidence and can trust myself. My secondary motives drive me:

- To avoid having to subject myself to others
- To have the power and to let myself count for something
- To stand up for myself and to prove my capabilities
- To be respected and to dominate the scene

- To have my own way and to be feared by others
- To be invulnerable.

My fear is that I am powerless and being controlled by others. My desire is to control situations and protect myself. That is why I focus on authority and action. The colour that suits me best is black/white (clear, absolute, no nuances).

My favourite leadership style is the Leader or Administrator. No wonder that they sometimes also call me the boss, fighter, assertive one or challenger.

Core qualities of an EIGHT

Positive characteristics of mine are: powerful, just, magnanimous, autonomous, honourable. I am direct, independent, courageous, strong, energetic and protective. My core qualities are: pugnacity, directness, courage and authority.

Less healthy aspects of an EIGHT

The less positive characteristics of an EIGHT are that he can be intimidating, blunt, egocentric and confrontational, sometimes also unrefined or unfeeling, dominating and even dictatorial or revengeful. He is allergic to infirmity and indecisiveness. Under his power and energy can be felt a current of lust. What he avoids is weakness. Where he can be obsessive is in retribution. His defence mechanism is denial, the literal blocking off and denial of vulnerable feelings. These are then simply (and temporarily) no

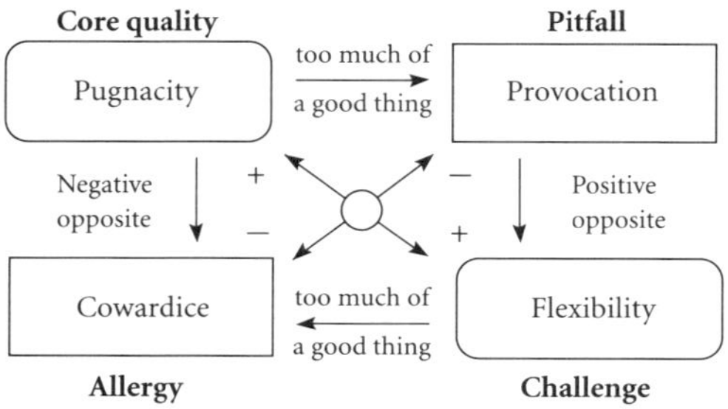
Core quality
Pugnacity
too much of a good thing
Pitfall
Provocation
Negative opposite
Positive opposite
Cowardice
too much of a good thing
Flexibility
Allergy
Challenge

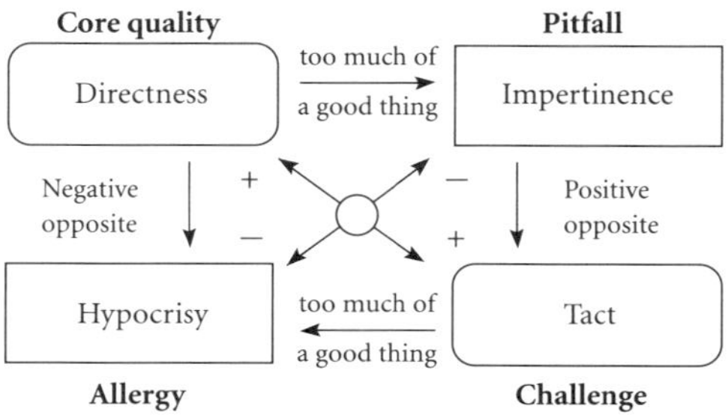
Core quality
Directness
too much of a good thing
Pitfall
Impertinence
Negative opposite
Positive opposite
Hypocrisy
too much of a good thing
Tact
Allergy
Challenge

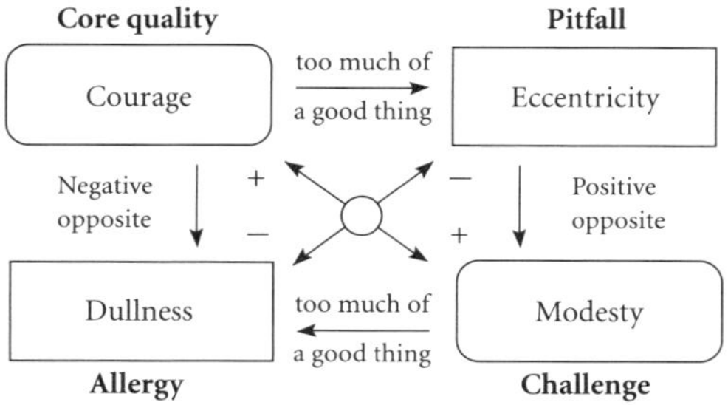
Core quality
Courage
too much of a good thing
Pitfall
Eccentricity
Negative opposite
Positive opposite
Dullness
too much of a good thing
Modesty
Allergy
Challenge

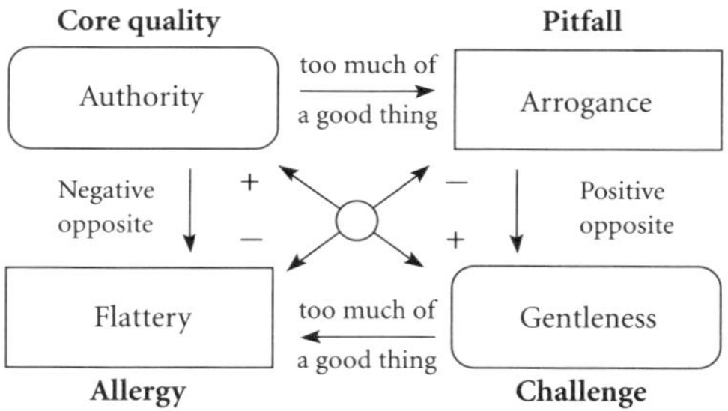
Core quality
Authority
too much of a good thing
Pitfall
Arrogance
Negative opposite
Positive opposite
Flattery
too much of a good thing
Gentleness
Allergy
Challenge

longer in the consciousness. This prevents an EIGHT from being aware of his vulnerability and his weaker sides.

Under pressure or stress the Leader tends to start displaying the less positive characteristics of the Observer. Under stress the EIGHT feels himself inferior and that makes his personality impassive and cold. As his strategy he chooses to withdraw in order to think. Then he can be unapproachable and socially inept. He can also be inculpatory, hostile and destructive in his behaviour, become distant, and begin to worry and have doubts. At his worst he is merciless and destroys everyone around him (including himself). The antidote that can help him most to break through worn-out patterns is innocence.

Wings of an EIGHT

A Leader with a SEVEN wing is more extrovert, more enterprising, more energetic, quicker and more egocentric. If a Leader has more NINE influences, then he is quieter, milder, more friendly, more receptive, and more orientated to harmony.

An EIGHT at his best

What gives a Leader a sense of fulfilment is having the reins in his hands and controlling life. When relaxed the Leader has access to the positive characteristics of the Helper. The TWO's compassion makes him more sociable, warmer and more human. He is more helpful and learns to put himself in another's place, be open for others and be more considerate. He is able to experience his own soft sides and accept them. He also dares to be vulnerable in attitude.

In his work he has learned to be aware of his impact on others. He uses his natural leadership qualities in a reasonable and responsible manner and is respected for this by his fellow workers. He has learned to know the value of harmony by mediating between opposing visions and reaching a consensus instead of imposing his will. An EIGHT who has learned to temper his power with compassion is only then truly powerful. At his best an EIGHT balances his power with concern, helpfulness and inspiration. He uses his power to help others and to be perceptive and sensitive to his own needs and those of others. Team members who are treated unfairly can count on the EIGHT's support. The Leader who has developed himself in the positive sense, is in contact with his softer sides and feelings. He dares to admit his vulnerability and learns to orientate himself more towards others than fight against them. He lets others have their say, listens more, instead of talking continually himself and being ready with his opinion. He acquires trust in the motives of others and can delegate better.

A healthy EIGHT has learned to deploy his power in the right way and for the right purposes.

Core quadrants and arrow movements of an EIGHT

The relationships an EIGHT has with his arrow movements can be summarised in the following three core quadrants.

Type Eight

Core quality: Courage — (+) → Unapproachability (**Pitfall**)
Courage — Negative opposite → Unapproachability
Unapproachability — Positive opposite → Spontaneity (**Challenge**)
Unapproachability — (−) → (too much of a good thing)

Core quality: Reflectiveness — (+) → Unapproachability (too much of a good thing)
Reflectiveness — Negative opposite → Emotionalism (**Allergy**)

Pitfall: Provocation — (−) → Modesty
Modesty — Positive opposite → (too much of a good thing) ↔ Caution (**Pitfall**)
Modesty — Negative opposite → Bluntness (**Allergy**)
Modesty — (+) / (−)

Caution — Positive opposite → Directness (**Challenge**)
Caution — (−) / (+)

TYPE EIGHT in balance gets the quality of TYPE TWO The Helper

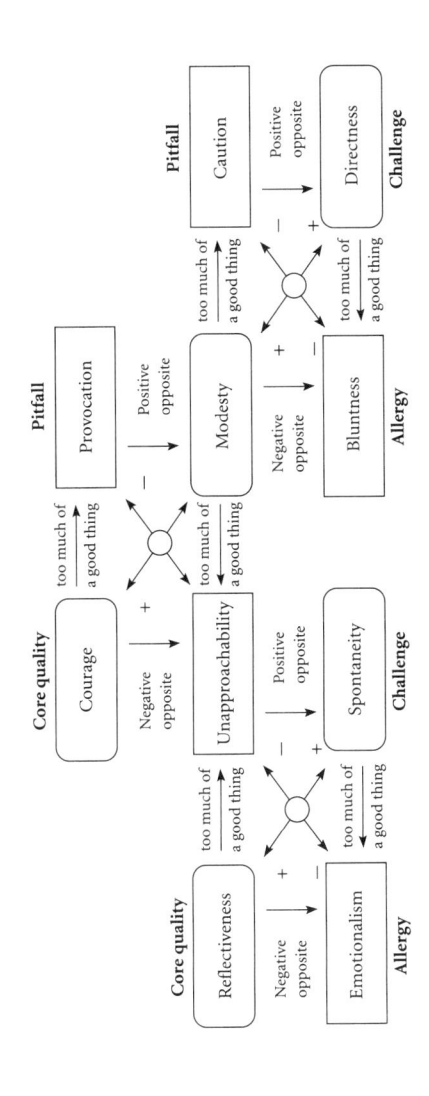

TYPE EIGHT under pressure gets the pitfall of TYPE FIVE The Observer

Type ❾ The Mediator

"If I get my meals on time then you won't hear me complain. No, really, I'm a contented person. I've now been 42 years in the shop, alone at first and for the last 30 years with my wife, and that still suits me down to the ground. It's very varied the work, isn't it? Every day is always different. Yes, that's the nice thing about this work, the variety. And when I shut the shop then it's time for my pigeons, eh?"

Mediator
9

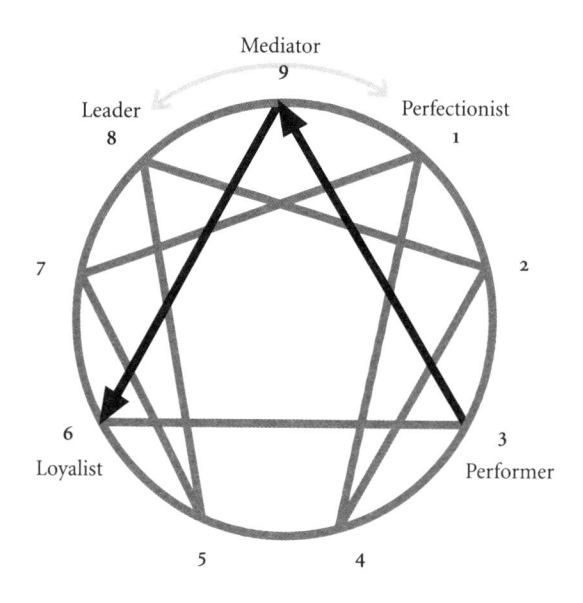

Leader
8

Perfectionist
1

7

2

6
Loyalist

3
Performer

5

4

General description of a NINE

I can oversee all standpoints. I do not like conflicts and my motto is: live and let live. I can simply reason away problems. I can be a little too lazy and take too much lying down. Sometimes I appear to be indecisive because I can see the advantages and disadvantages of all the options. Usually I can get along with everyone. I hate having to rush or having others put pressure on me. I like it if everyone is content. I often have difficulty in starting something. But once I have begun, I keep going. When I am very busy I tend to divide my attention and start doing unimportant things.

Detailed description of a NINE

I stand in another's shoes without thinking. I am sensible of everything, all the various standpoints. In discussions I always try to reconcile the diverging opinions with each other. That sometimes makes it awkward for me to make a choice. Every choice shuts a door. I also find decisions about my own life difficult. Often I never finish the journey inside myself. Then I say to myself: Let it be, we'll see. But if I've made my choice, then I don't let myself be budged from it. Sometimes I don't reach the stage of doing things because I fritter away my energy. Give me options, and particularly for things I don't want. I often know better what I don't want than what I do want. I can scrap things. Actually everything is all right; I am content.

Intuitively I can put myself in someone's place very well and experience what goes on inside others. The danger of this is that I am sometimes busier with what others experience and want than with my own inner self.

With conflicts I tend to pull myself back. When I don't agree with something, I sometimes show that indirectly in unruliness. The saying 'To be silent is to approve' does not apply to me. If I say nothing, it certainly does not mean that I agree. People can better ask me what my opinion is. In a group my silence can be a powerful tool. I can also employ delaying tactics if someone is in a hurry. I can keep denying with great obstinacy that conflicts exist or that something is wrong. When I get moving I can commit myself fully to something.

Inside me there is great energy and many emotions. Even so I am usually calm and quiet. At least on the surface. I spend a good deal of energy in staying the master of my emotions. I do not readily show my anger, but if it happens then it really happens. I regret it almost immediately. Why do I let myself be thrown off my balance? Why do I get so wound up? I smooth over all the anger and resentment inside me. I like it when my life ripples along. I think people who find themselves important are ridiculous. What is there that is really important? Artificiality, pompousness and humbug make me almost physically ill. I like to bring things back to their proper proportions. Cynicism is not unknown to me. Growth means for me taking responsibility for my own life—not letting things take their own course and sink with the attitude: 'It all doesn't matter'.

In my vision of life my viewpoint is that everything will be all right if we stay calm, friendly and united with one another. The most important values I stand for are love and harmony.

I am convinced that harmony between people ensures that the organisation gets along well. I often ask myself such questions as: What are the viewpoints of others and how can I concur with them so that no tension arises?

All my attention is directed at possible claims from those around me. My image of myself is: I am content.

My primary motivation is that I want to live in unity and harmony with others. My secondary motives drive me:
- To strive for and maintain harmony and peace
- To mediate in conflicts and bring people together
- To keep things and maintain them as they are
- Not to admit that I am confused by something
- To avoid tension and conflicts or to minimalise them
- To deny the existence of everything that is difficult to accept or difficult to handle.

Diagram 1:

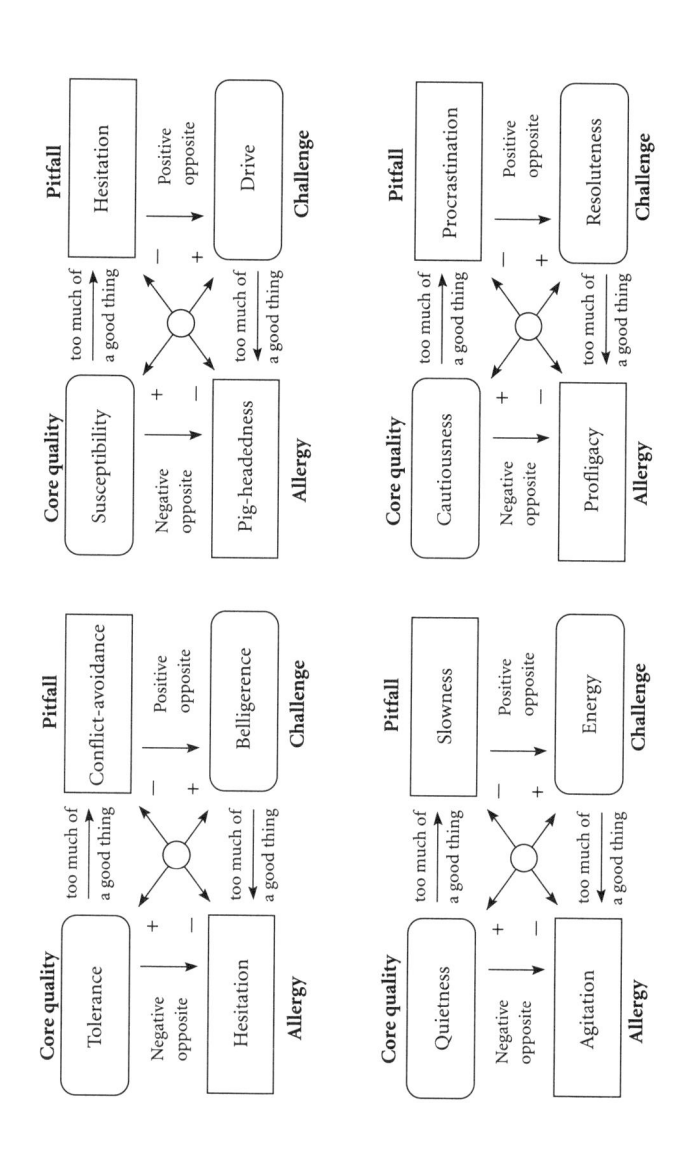

Core quality: **Tolerance** —(+)→ Allergy: **Hesitation** (Negative opposite)

Pitfall: **Conflict-avoidance** —(Positive opposite)→ Challenge: **Belligerence**

too much of a good thing (−) / too much of a good thing (+)

Diagram 2:

Core quality: **Susceptibility** —(+)→ Allergy: **Pig-headedness** (Negative opposite)

Pitfall: **Hesitation** —(Positive opposite)→ Challenge: **Drive**

too much of a good thing (−) / too much of a good thing (+)

Diagram 3:

Core quality: **Quietness** —(+)→ Allergy: **Agitation** (Negative opposite)

Pitfall: **Slowness** —(Positive opposite)→ Challenge: **Energy**

too much of a good thing (−) / too much of a good thing (+)

Diagram 4:

Core quality: **Cautiousness** —(+)→ Allergy: **Profligacy** (Negative opposite)

Pitfall: **Procrastination** —(Positive opposite)→ Challenge: **Resoluteness**

too much of a good thing (−) / too much of a good thing (+)

My fear is that I am unloved and being separated from others. I long for love, union and stability with others. That is why I focus on agreement, harmony and routine. The colour that suits me is gold (searching, peaceful and harmonious). My favourite leadership style is the Reconciler.

No wonder that they sometimes also call me peacemaker, negotiator, preserver or even the saint.

Core qualities of a NINE

Positive characteristics of mine are: patient, diplomatic, a good negotiator, reassuring and content. I can be modest, harmonious, accepting, steady and sensible. My core qualities are: tolerance, quietness, cautiousness and susceptibility.

Less healthy aspects of a NINE

The less positive characteristics of a NINE are that he is a procrastinator, easily distracted, dull, soothing, forgetful and indecisive. He is allergic to aggression and instability. Under his diplomacy emotional sloth can sometimes be felt. What he avoids is conflict and where he can become obsessive is in always adapting himself. His defence mechanism is self-anaesthesia. In order not to experience feelings of anger, a NINE lets his anger fall asleep. He finds an escape in doing unimportant things and letting his attention be diluted. This prevents a NINE from being conscious of annoying feelings within himself and conflicts.

Under pressure or stress the Mediator tends to display the less positive characteristics of the Loyalist. He can become indecisive and suspicious. He can also make himself over-dependent on rules and become afraid. A stressed Mediator worries, has many doubts and becomes active with difficulty. The antidote that can help him most to break through worn-out patterns is right action.

Wings of a NINE

A Mediator with a strong EIGHT wing is more extrovert, more assertive and more anti-authoritarian, more decisive and readier to deal with conflict. A Mediator with a ONE wing is orientated more towards doing things well. A strong ONE wing makes him more orderly, more critical, more formal and more compliant.

A NINE at his best

What gives a Mediator a feeling of fulfilment is having been able to make a contribution to peace and harmony. When relaxed the Mediator has access to the positive characteristics of the Performer. When he feels sure of himself he can stipulate his own ideas and positions. He acquires the energy to act and he can solve conflicts in a constructive manner. He becomes purposeful, effective, active, motivating and enthusiastic. He can set priorities, make choices and present himself better.

In his work a NINE is concerned with unanimity among different people and opinions and so finds solutions that can be accepted by the majority. He learns to trust his inner power through confrontation and non-avoidance of difficulties. Developing his assertiveness and standing up for his own viewpoints and plans are important steps. He has learned to be pro-active in establishing goals and priorities and to take the right steps in order to achieve the desired result. At his best he mediates constructively among conflicts while he maintains his own standpoint.

His capacity to identify himself with divergent viewpoints makes him an effective negotiator. Jobs are assigned in clear and detailed form. Because he finds that a team in harmony is effective, team members are urged to work with each other in concord, instead of competing with each other. He can say to himself: I am successful.

A healthy NINE has learned to proceed from a personal position.

Core quadrants and arrow movements of a NINE

The relationships a NINE has with his arrow movements can be summarised in the following three core quadrants. (See figure on next page.)

Type Nine

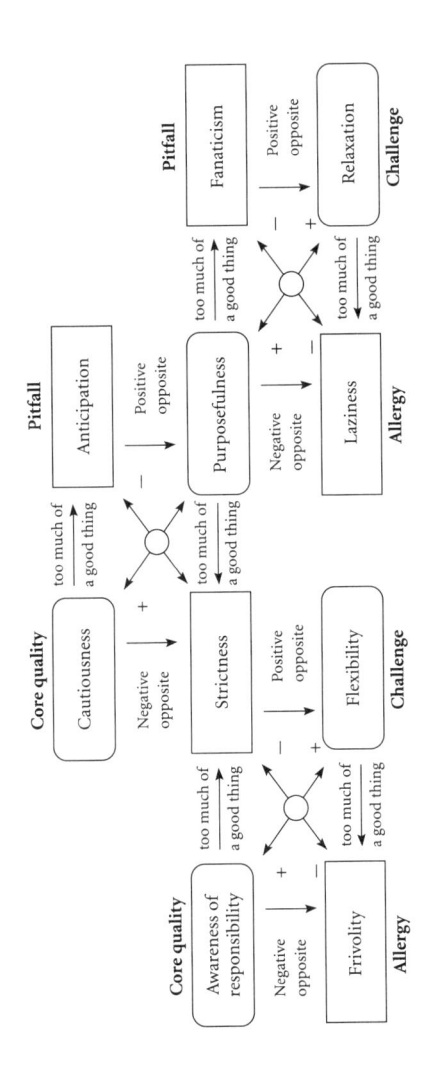

Core quality: Cautiousness → (too much of a good thing) → **Strictness** (Pitfall: Anticipation — Positive opposite → Purposefulness)

Cautiousness — Negative opposite → Strictness
Strictness — Positive opposite → **Flexibility** (Challenge)

Purposefulness — Negative opposite → **Laziness** (Allergy)
Purposefulness — (too much of a good thing) → **Fanaticism** (Pitfall) — Positive opposite → **Relaxation** (Challenge)

Core quality: Awareness of responsibility — Negative opposite → **Frivolity** (Allergy)
Awareness of responsibility — (too much of a good thing) → Strictness

Type NINE under pressure gets the pitfall of TYPE SIX The Loyalist

Type NINE in balance gets the quality of TYPE THREE The Performer

134

A test
Development Plans
Grass

A test

THE STATEMENTS on pages 138–146 apply to the nine enneagram types. Read them carefully and indicate the score. Don't think too much about it. Your first inspiration is often the best.

It is normal for you to recognise something of every type. The most accurate way to respond is as how you were as a young adult. That is certainly the case when you have done a lot for your personal development. When you have undergone significant changes, it is important for you to identify yourself with the person you were before these changes.

Remember that no one type is better or worse than another. The ideal is to become the best 'you' that you can be. Be sure to be honest with yourself in answering the questions and try not to choose something that you would like to be.

How much of the Perfectionist applies to me?

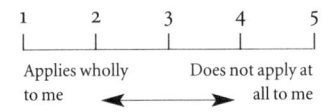

```
1      2      3      4      5
|_____|_____|_____|_____|
Applies wholly      Does not apply at
to me      ←——→      all to me
```

                                                                             Score

- I find it important to do things well ...
- I am critical of myself and others ...
- I ask a lot of myself ...
- I attach a lot of importance to thoroughness ...
- I let myself be guided by my principles and ideals ...
- I find order important ...
- I do more than others expect of me ...
- I find it very irritating to waste time ...
- It bothers me that things are not as they should be ...
- I would rather do everything myself, then I know for sure it is done well ...
- I have a kind of inner list of what may and what may not ...
- I take responsibility seriously ...
- I am very sensitive to signs of appreciation, in other words I 'cherish' them ...

                                                                             ——— +

                                              Total score Perfectionist ...

Copyright © 2001 Eclectica, Oudenbosch

How much of the Helper applies to me?

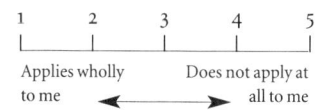

```
1       2       3       4       5
|———————|———————|———————|———————|
Applies wholly          Does not apply at
to me         ◄——————►  all to me
```

                                                                                                Score

- I find it difficult to say no ...
- I have the tendency to do as others please ...
- I like giving people advice ...
- I have a strong need for intimacy ...
- I attach importance to my (outward) appearance and good taste ...
- I have difficulty in dealing with rejection ...
- It makes me feel good when I can help another ...
- I lay more emphasis on how I feel than on what I do ...
- I have a warm, friendly personality ...
- I find it difficult to reject directly someone who is important to me ...
- I find emotional questions important ...
- I like to feel a bond with people who are important to me ...
- I have the tendency to do too much for others ...

                                                                                             ——— +

                                Total score Helper ...

Copyright © 2001 Eclectica, Oudenbosch

How much of the Performer applies to me?

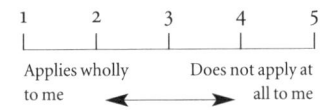

```
1       2       3       4       5
|———————|———————|———————|———————|
Applies wholly      Does not apply at
to me      ←——→      all to me
```

                                                               Score

- I like winning ...
- I attach great value to being successful ...
- I am good at organising things efficiently ...
- I am pragmatic by nature; 'what do I get out of it' is an important question for me ...
- I am a self-confident go-getter ...
- I can adapt easily to every situation ...
- I like recognition ...
- I find it important to make a good impression ...
- I become impatient when people do not move as fast as I want ...
- I hate it when something I do doesn't work ...
- I can identify myself so much with my work or role that I forget who I really am ...
- I like it when people admire me ...
- I have difficulty in dealing with failures ...

———— +

Total score Performer ...

Copyright © 2001 Eclectica, Oudenbosch

How much of the Individualist applies to me?

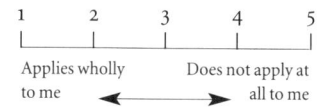

```
1       2       3       4       5
|———————|———————|———————|———————|
Applies wholly        Does not apply at
to me         ◄——————►     all to me
```

	Score
– I attach great value to authenticity	…
– I feel different from others	…
– I like depth, deep subjects (life and death)	…
– I feel misunderstood	…
– I long for the unattainable	…
– I feel drawn to everything that is intense	…
– I focus myself on the essence of things	…
– I am swung to and fro between ups and downs	…
– I am very sensitive	…
– I like to do things differently, in my own way	…
– I hate everyday dullness	…
– I am searching for the meaning of existence	…
– I am attracted to symbols	…
	——— +
Total score Individualist	…

Copyright © 2001 Eclectica, Oudenbosch

How much of the Observer applies to me?

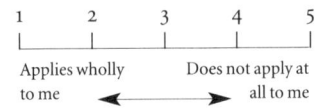

```
1      2      3      4      5
|      |      |      |      |
Applies wholly        Does not apply at
to me      ◄──────►   all to me
```

                                                     Score

- I withdraw when I become too susceptible ...
- I have a strong need for autonomy ...
- I can be cynical ...
- I find it annoying when others meddle in my private affairs ...
- I have difficulty in sharing my feelings and emotions with people ...
- I need a lot of time and space for myself to think things over ...
- I find it important to understand things ...
- I find it difficult to react when I don't understand something ...
- I can consider things clearly and logically ...
- I prefer to keep my feelings to myself ...
- I am stingy with my time ...
- I am sometimes accused of being distant ...
- I can easily lose my sense of time when I am concentrating on something ...

———+

                                    Total score Observer ...

Copyright © 2001 Eclectica, Oudenbosch

How much of the Loyalist applies to me?

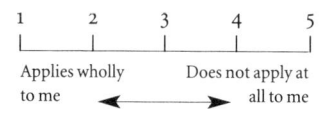

```
1       2       3       4       5
|-------|-------|-------|-------|
Applies wholly      Does not apply at
to me        ←——→      all to me
```

	Score
– I find it important to know things for certain	...
– I have a keen eye for things that can go wrong	...
– I have a sort of sixth sense for sniffing out danger	...
– I abhor ambiguity	...
– I like clarity	...
– I find loyalty very important	...
– I want to know everything in order to be sure	...
– I find it important to make the right decision	...
– I like to be sure of myself before I take action	...
– I like to have a framework in which to work	...
– I have the tendency to think about how things can go wrong	...
– I am careful because I am afraid that others will judge me wrongly	...
– I protect myself against the criticism of others	...
	——— +
Total score Loyalist	...

Copyright © 2001 Eclectica, Oudenbosch

How much of the Optimist applies to me?

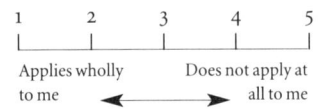

```
1      2      3      4      5
|——————|——————|——————|——————|
Applies wholly       Does not apply at
to me         ←——→    all to me
```

                                                              Score

- I hate negativeness ...
- I get over a loss quickly ...
- I don't like obligations ...
- I am busy with many things at the same time and I plan ahead ...
- I hate routine if it limits me ...
- I cannot imagine a life without options ...
- I change my opinion easily when I have a better option ...
- I look on the sunny side of life; I am a born optimist ...
- I like telling stories ...
- I am a real epicurean ...
- I wish people were a little more light-hearted ...
- I am not easily caught out ...
- I stop something when I no longer like doing it ...

                                                                     —— +

                              Total score Optimist ...

Copyright © 2001 Eclectica, Oudenbosch

How much of the Leader applies to me?

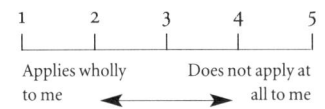

```
1     2     3     4     5
|_____|_____|_____|_____|
Applies wholly      Does not apply at
to me      ←——→    all to me
```

	Score
– I find it important to be strong	…
– I have the tendency to dominate	…
– I make my own rules	…
– I don't allow myself to be weak and to show my vulnerability	…
– I get what I want	…
– I feel where someone's weak points lie	…
– I demand honesty	…
– I respect power in others	…
– I have an aversion to authority being exercised over me	…
– I sense who has the power in a group	…
– I can stand up for myself very well and fight for what I want	…
– I want to be my own boss and like doing things my own way	…
– I provoke people, draw them out of their shells, in order to test them	…
	——— +
Total score Leader	…

Copyright © 2001 Eclectica, Oudenbosch

How much of the Mediator applies to me?

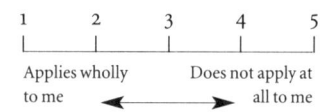

```
1      2      3      4      5
|------|------|------|------|
Applies wholly      Does not apply at
to me      ◄——————►    all to me
```

                                                   Score

- I avoid conflicts ...
- I like to determine my own tempo ...
- I find harmony important ...
- I like being sociable ...
- I find it irritating when people around me goad me ...
- I divide my attention and sometimes cannot concentrate well as a result ...
- I can absorb many points of view ...
- I have difficulty in defining my own limits ...
- I find it irritating when someone disturbs my peace ...
- I find that most people work themselves up too much about things ...
- I don't get angry easily ...
- I don't demand much of others ...
- I let someone have his way easier than making a scene about it ...

                                                     ——— +

                            Total score Mediator ...

Copyright © 2001 Eclectica, Oudenbosch

The scores give an indication of the extent to which your characteristics correspond with an enneagram number. Also which characteristics of types you do not or barely recognise in yourself. The type with the highest score can be your basic number. But that need not be so. As your knowledge of the enneagram grows, you will discover how it is possible for you to score highly with other numbers while these are still not your basic enneagram number.

The test is a starting-point for discovering and understanding yourself. Your highest score usually indicates your basic type. Even so your second or third highest score can finally turn out to be your enneagram type. So use the test as an indicator. When you score highly in more than one type then read the personal descriptions to find out which fits you best.

	Total score
Perfectionist (page 138):	...
Helper (page 139):	...
Performer (page 140):	...
Individualist (page 141):	...
Observer (page 142):	...
Loyalist (page 143):	...
Optimist (page 144):	...
Leader (page 145):	...
Mediator (page 146):	...

Development Plans

As already said in the Foreword, our aim on the one hand is to increase awareness of yourself and, on the other hand, to convert this awareness into concrete action. For this reason the accompanying CD-ROM is aimed at making a personal development plan. If you would like to do this then you can go through the following nine steps, which you will also find on the CD-ROM. Look at it as a kind of a chapter list for your personal development plan, your PDP.

Chapter 1 *Where do I come from?*
Chapter 2 *What has helped me to become who I am?*
Chapter 3 *Who am I?*
Chapter 4 *Why am I here?*
Chapter 5 *What is the thread in my life?*
Chapter 6 *What do I want?*
Chapter 7 *What gives me energy?*
Chapter 8 *What are my motives?*
Chapter 9 *How do I handle it?*

CHAPTER 1 *Where do I come from?*

Here you concentrate on gathering as much information as possible.

1. Personal information
   - Personalia with personal information
   - My nest: notes on the family situation in which I grew up.
2. History
   - Baby, infant, elementary school; notable facts from the first 12 years of my life.
   - Puberty and adolescence; important facts from the period 12 to 21 years old.
3. Still farther back
   - Memories as foetus in the womb.
   - Memories of former lives?

Why is this the first step? Because Type ONE in the enneagram, the Perfectionist, likes completeness and thoroughness. He always begins at the beginning, keeping his feelings out of range in the meantime. He is self-disciplined, organised, orderly and conscientious. Thus he begins at the beginning with gathering facts.

Chapter 2 *What has helped me to become who I am?*
Here pose yourself the following questions:
1. People
   - Which people in the past have played an important role in my life until now?
   - Which people are important now in my life?
2. Experiences
   - Which positive experiences have contributed to me becoming who I am now?
   - Which painful or negative experiences have contributed to me becoming who I am now?
3. Sources of help
   - Which qualities in myself have helped me to become who I am now?
   - If you have the idea that an invisible something or someone (a guardian angel?) has helped you, how did you experience that?

Why is this the second step? Because Type two in the enneagram, the Helper, tends to help others and is less occupied with what he needs. He is acquiescent, helpful, supportive and considerate. What a two needs is to consider what has helped him. And perhaps even more important, how he has helped himself, and can help himself in future.

Chapter 3 *Who am I?*

Here you go in search of your basis centre, your enneagram type and your core qualities. It is time to go somewhat deeper and search for what makes you unique.

Why is this the third step? Because Type THREE in the enneagram, the Performer, more than anyone, ought to ask himself this question. He is enthusiastic, purposeful, competent, efficient and sure of himself. He has difficulty doing nothing and has so far the tendency to be busy all the time that a little reflection would do him no harm.

Chapter 4 *Why am I here?*

In this step you search for the meaning of your life, the 'why'.

1. Mission
   - What is my mission in life?
   - What do I have to do in this life?
2. Meaning
   - What makes my life meaningful?
   - When should my life be worthwhile?
3. Added value
   - What is the added value of my life for myself and my environment?
   - What would I like people to say about me at my funeral?

Why is this the fourth step? Because Type four in the enneagram, the Individualist, always asks himself this sort of question. He is sensitive, original and creative, and fond of introspection. He abhors the ordinary, the everyday, and aims constantly at experiencing everything deeply. For him it is all about authenticity and connection with people.

Chapter 5 *What is the thread in my life?*

In this phase you go in search of coherence, of patterns in your life, by asking yourself the following questions:

1. Events
   - Which events constantly repeat themselves in my life?
   - Which events around me continually move me anew?
2. Patterns
   - What do I encounter in myself again and again?
   - What lesson do I keep having to learn?
3. Development
   - What development do I see?
   - How have I changed in the course of time?

Why is this the fifth step? Because Type five in the enneagram, the Observer, likes analysing. By understanding he gains an overall view and that gives him a feeling of safety, because knowing everything gives security. Only if he understands something can he act. That means that he reflects a lot. He stores everything up and tries to classify information. For him all the pieces must fit together. He is continually looking for the key to being able to understand.

Chapter 6 *What do I want?*

Here the question of wishes arises. What would you really want of yourself, what do you wish for? Just make a list of the things you would really like. In this the challenges of your enneagram type, your wings and arrows and your core quadrants can help you.

Why is this the sixth step? Because Type six in the enneagram, the Loyalist, from a great sense of duty, tends to direct his attention out towards everything that can go wrong. He is watchful, serious and fair, but he can have doubts about himself and what he wants. Then he can become unsure and orientate himself particularly towards what people expect of him, instead of deciding himself what he wants. Thus, for a six, the question 'What do I want?' is a challenge.

Chapter 7 *What gives me energy?*

Before you convert your wishes into actions and deeds, it can be useful to ask first what sort of things get your motor running. In this step we are concerned with energy and enthusiasm. What are you prepared to make an effort for and spend your life's energy on? What gets you out of bed in the morning?

1. Passion
   - What rouses my interest?
   - What makes my heart beat faster?
2. Pleasure
   - What makes me enthusiastic?
   - What bores me?
3. Energy
   - What would I not miss for anything?
   - What am I prepared to make sacrifices for?

Why is this the seventh step? Because Type SEVEN in the enneagram, the Optimist, is always on the lookout for excitement and pleasure. He has a very active spirit that jumps quickly back and forth between different ideas. He is cheerful as long as he can do what he wants, and is always open to new ideas. Playfulness, sparkle and zest for life are part of him, just like spontaneity, curiosity and light-heartedness. He has no shortage of energy.

Chapter 8 *What are my motives?*

Step eight is the penultimate one. Here you look for your motives and your limits.

1. Motives
   - What are inner motives for paying attention to my development?
   - What are external motives for paying attention to my development?
2. Values
   - Which values are important for me?
   - Why are these values so important?
3. Limits
   - What are my limits?
   - Where do I make no concessions?

Why is this the eighth step? Because, for Type EIGHT in the enneagram, the Leader, influence and power are the themes which occupy him. He is powerful, independent, pugnacious and courageous. His authority gains strength if he learns to use his power in the right way and for the right goals. Thus he will have to get to know what drives him in order to discover his true motivation.

Grass

'The grass doesn't grow faster if you pull on it.'

AND THERE YOU ARE, then, with all these insights into yourself. It seems logical for you to ask: 'What must I do now?' Many people think—after they have discovered their enneagram types and core qualities—that they have to start working hard on their challenge. Thus the Mediator tries very hard to take up his own position, or the Optimist tries to be content with just one thing, only to find out that he gets more and more frustrated. Many have done the same. Many people try hard to work on themselves and to change themselves: to become a better adviser, leader, father and husband. Alas—or perhaps happily—it doesn't work that way.

You can certainly change, but not by working hard on yourself. It is actually much more difficult, although it doesn't seem so in the first instance. In one way or another 'working hard on yourself' maintains the illusion that a greater effort guarantees a better result. We are brought up this way, nearly everybody thinks this way. But the laws of growth and development work differently. Growth will not be forced, no matter how hard you work. Growth can be stimulated, but it has its own tempo. That applies also to development. Somewhere in the past we have forgotten something important, or left it behind. From that moment on there have been but two possibilities: either you work hard on yourself, or you do nothing. What we have forgotten is the third option 'not doing', something quite different from 'doing nothing'. 'Not doing' means that you are there and very alert, observing and not acting, but letting 'be'.

Thus three steps emerge which start inner growth:

1 You become aware of the dynamic that belongs to your type and your core quadrants. Working with the enneagram and core qualities helps you to understand all that is involved. Without this awareness you have no idea why you do what you do. This step is concerned first and foremost with observing.

2 The second step is taking responsibility for your inner imbalance by facing the fact that you are not perfect and that you are not just a type who has core qualities, but that you are also their shadowy sides. This step is more difficult than it seems, because we often secretly still want to be perfect. The main point here is to make room within yourself for imperfection.

3 The last step is not only to face up to your imperfection, but also to learn to love it and embrace it. This is perhaps the most important step of all and the most difficult for everyone. It actually means accepting pain as part of life. It means embracing with compassion and feeling your own imbalance, shadow, pitfalls, irritations and the consequent destructiveness.

At the moment you do that, you have immediate access to your challenge and to the characteristics belonging to the arrow movement when you are relaxed. You cannot work on this; you can acquire it only by learning to love yourself.

Anna Terruwe put that into words as follows:

> *'You may be as you are*
> *in order to be who you are*
> *but cannot be yet*
> *and you may become it*
> *in your way and in your time.'*

This loving attitude towards yourself, towards others, towards organisations and towards the environment is what we wish for you.

May the core qualities of yourself and the enneagram help you to attain it.

Contact addresses

Daniel Ofman
Kern Konsult BV
Organisation development
Beerensteinerlaan 24
1406 NS Bussum
The Netherlands
Tel: (+31) (0)35- 693.54.45
Fax: (+31) (0)35- 602.26.26
e-mail: dofman@euronet.nl
Internet: www.kernkonsult.nl
Internet: www.ofman.nl
For training in Core qualities
you can contact Kern Konsult

Rita van der Weck
Eclectica
Entstraat 29
4731 XH Oudenbosch
The Netherlands
Tel: (+31) (0)165 –31.39.52
Fax: (+31) (0)165–52.05.33
e-mail: spunk@wxs.nl
For training in the Enneagram
you can contact Eclectica